FACILITATION SKILLS

Helping Groups Make Decisions

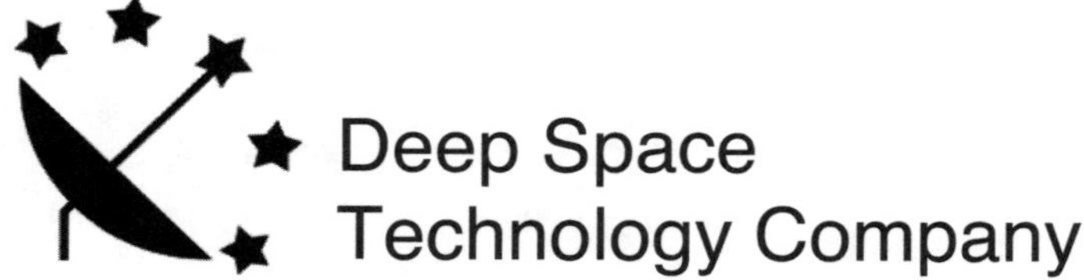
Deep Space
Technology Company

Personal Leadership SERIES

Facilitation Skills

Helping Groups Make Decisions

Gregory B. Putz

Simple Steps to Help Groups & Teams
Focus on the Issue and
Build Agreement on Solutions

2nd Edition

Visit our websites at
http://deepspacetechnology.com
http://dstcx.com

ATTENTION: SCHOOLS AND CORPORATIONS
Deep Space Technology Company books are available at quantity discounts with bulk purchase for education, business, or sales promotional use. For information, please write to: SPECIAL SALES DEPARTMENT, DEEP SPACE TECHNOLOGY COMPANY, P.O. BOX 802, BOUNTIFUL, UT 84011-802

ISBN 0-9664456-1-9
Second Edition, First Printing

Printed in the United States of America

Library of Congress Cataloging-in-Publication Data

Putz, Gregory B. (Gregory Bryan), 1952-
Facilitation skills : helping groups make decisions / Gregory B. Putz. -- 1st ed.
p. cm.
Includes bibliographical references (p.) and index.
ISBN 0-9664456-1-9 (pbk.)
1. Teams in the workplace. 2. Decision making. 3. Group facilitation. I. Title.
HD66.P88 1998
658.3' 128--dc21 98-25716
CIP

Published by Deep Space Technology Company

Deep Space Technology Company
P.O. Box 802
Bountiful, UT 84011-0802
(801) 292-1307 Fax (801) 292-0378
www.deepspacetechnology.com
www.dstcx.com

Facilitation Skills

CONTENTS

I. The Big Picture

1 The Facilitation Process

2 Your Job As Facilitator

3 The Role Of The Participants

II. Steps For Successful Facilitation

4 What's The **Issue**?

5 What Are Our **Concerns**?

6 Any Possible **Solutions**?

7 Our **Criteria**?

8 What's Our **Action**?

9 **Check**?

III. Doing It!

10 Getting **Started**

11 You And The **Leader**

12 Pre-Meeting **Logistics** & The Room

13 **Flipcharts** And Other Visual Tools

14 The **First** Meeting

IV. Helping You With...

15 Building **Consensus**

16 Handling **Conflict**

17 Getting **Participation**

18 Building **Trust**

19 Managing Your **Stress**

V. Appendices

20 Do's & Don'ts

21 Frequently-Asked Questions

22 Selected Resources

23 Examples You Can Use

24 Index

Everyone
is
Welcome to Participate!

ABOUT THE AUTHOR

Gregory Putz grew up on Miramar Avenue in Montecito, a small town several miles southeast of Santa Barbara, California. He spent his summer days at Miramar Beach, Hammond's Beach, and East Beach. Although he loved the fun and sun, his favorite activity was the annual summer weeklong backpacking trip with BSA Troop 33 to the Lyle Fork of the Tuolumne River in Yosemite National Park. What a bucolic life! How he eventually came to write books and facilitate corporate, church, and community groups, no one will ever know.

After graduating from Santa Barbara High School, Greg went north to attend college at the University of California in Berkeley. His favorite class was Subject A. He spent his first year in a Putnam Hall but escaped dormitory life when he found refuge in a social fraternity, Sigma Nu. After three years at the fraternity's Beta Psi chapter, he graduated with a Bachelor of Science degree in civil engineering (he would have majored in mechanical engineering but he couldn't fathom the obtuseness of thermodynamics). The following year, Greg received his Master of Science degree from the same department at Cal.

Greg joined the engineering division of a very large California oil company. He received his registration as a Professional Engineer in California. Soon afterwards, he married his college sweetheart, Suzanne They moved to Utah to escape the California crowds, congestion, and confusion. Within the year two beautiful baby daughters, Caroline and Danielle, were born. Life had returned to the halcyon days of Montecito.

Oil company engineering design and construction assignments yielded to operations, supervision, and human resources opportunities. Greg was soon teaching and facilitating work groups and teams in the area of problem solving. He expanded his work to facilitating countless other business, church, and civic groups within the Salt Lake City community.

Greg remains a steadfast believer in the creative powers of groups and their abilities to solve problems. He has experienced the satisfaction of seeing many, many groups arrive at wonderful solutions to complex problems. And that satisfaction is the reason for writing this book... he wished to share the secrets with you!

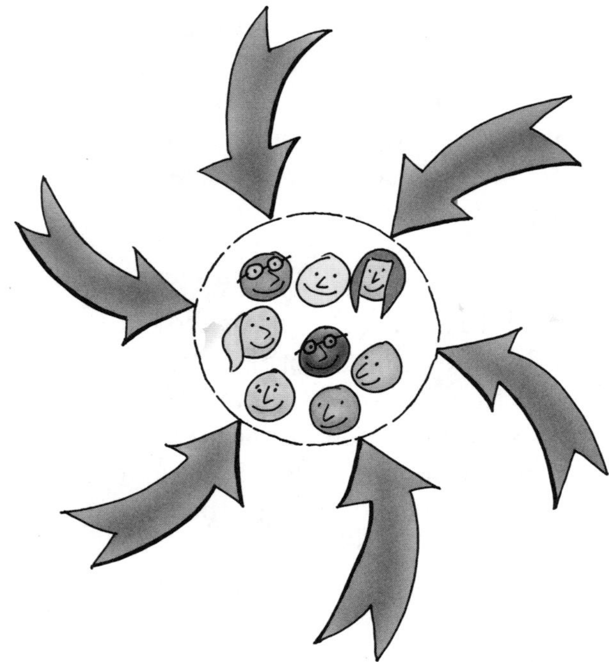

PREFACE - 1st Edition

Why do we need facilitation?

Because it enables any group to unlock the answers they are seeking. Those answers are the typically the root of change, either in a business or in some social unit.

Unfortunately, society has encouraged an opposite approach. The popularity of individualism has discouraged active, group problem solving. Frequently, it is viewed as a weakness when one person seeks group involvement in selecting solutions.

Also, an individual or group typically waits for someone else to cause a change. This behavior is reinforced from childhood throughout our adult lives. If a solution exists then someone will give it to us. If change is to occur then someone else will initiate it. We are therefore conditioned to be reactive not proactive.

As a result, too often we look for change coming from the outside in... or from the top down. We typically wait for others to solve our problems. But to be truly successful, we must instead look within ourselves to find the true source of change. Simply said, the answers are within us.

This book helps find those answers.

As more businesses strive to become high performance organizations they will depend more and more upon the creative abilities of their employees. As competitive pressures increase so will the demands upon employee work groups to develop and implement innovative solutions.

The traditional manager or supervisor can no longer provide answers to all the questions and demands of today's work place. With the technical nature of business expanding so quickly, it will difficult for a manager to keep up. Simply said, tomorrow's manager or supervisor will not be able to solve every problem at the office. Business will increasingly rely on employee teams and work groups to implement innovative solutions to solve company problems.

And it will be the facilitation skills of both supervisors and non-supervisory employees that extract these innovation solutions from the work groups. Instead of the historically passive, directed work groups, business will see the evolution of proactive, responsible ones. Such evolving work groups will require the services of neutral facilitators to help them unlock their creative solutions.

This book shows how to do that. It provides both the process and insights necessary for any person to act as a neutral facilitator. This book outlines a step-by-step approach on how to help a work group unlock its creative abilities while maintaining a safe, positive atmosphere.

You need to study this book and apply its processes if you want to harness the creativity and innovation of your employees! The old days of command and control management are quickly disappearing. This book will give you the ability to help your work group focus on the issues, make decisions, and gain support for their actions! Why not start helping them today?

- *Gregory Bryan Putz*
Bountiful, Utah
February 1998

PREFACE - 2nd Edition

It has been more than four years since the first edition was published... and I've learned some new tricks. Many of these new tools surfaced during my participation at work in a three-year program involving our facility's transition to a "high performance organization." This cultural shift focused on learning new skills, accepting new responsibilities, and breaking old paradigms about employee/workteam roles in the workplace. Each required group facilitation to identify issues, establish decision criteria, and agree on innovative solutions to doing business cheaper, better, and more reliably. You'll see these new facilitation tools in the five new chapters in Section IV, "Helping You With..." of this second edition.

I've also had the opportunity to attend addition seminars across the United States in facilitation and human performance/leadership areas. I have been very impressed with the seminars offered by the Disney Institute in Lake Buena Vista, Florida. Located at Walt Disney World, these classes have provided me with new insight and methods to stimulate group involvement and openness in facilitation sessions. I'll share those new tools with you in Chapters 17 & 18, "Getting Participation," and "Building Trust."

In addition, this second edition has an expanded Chapter 22, "Selected Resources," as well as a new

Chapter 23, "Examples You Can Use." Both chapters provide you with additional information on group dynamics, graphic & visual tools, and the facilitation process.

I hope that you will benefit from the insights and tools of this book. After four years of conducting a seemly endless number of problem-solving sessions, I believe, more strongly than ever before, that groups and workteams have a fantastic power to arrive at powerful solutions to difficult problems. Your skills as a facilitator will help them do it!

Thanks for reading my book.

- *Gregory Putz*
Bountiful, Utah
March 2002

Thanks to

Suzie... for her patience
Caroline... for her optimism
Danielle... for her wit
Curt Last... for his perspective
Jim Newton... for his high ideals
Dennis Green... for his positive energy

Respect the dignity,
the worth,
and
the creative potential
of
every human being
in the
organization.

I

The Big Picture

1. The Facilitation Process
2. Your Job As Facilitator
3. The Role Of The Participants

"Tell a man there are 300 billion stars in the universe and he'll believe you.
Tell him a bench has wet paint on it and he'll have to touch it to be sure."

— **Murphy**

> "The sun never shines on a cause of greater worth."
> — **Thomas Paine**

1 THE FACILITATION PROCESS

Why bother with this process? Facilitation means to "free from obstacles" and to "make easier." So, why facilitate? Why spend the extra time and energy to follow a detailed, step-by-step process? Thirty years ago it was unheard of. Ten years ago it was a rarity. Today, facilitation is a popular process in identifying problems, resolving misunderstandings, building consensus, and creating action plans around important issues and problems. Facilitation provides solutions that everyone in a group can support — and with such support, solutions having a greater chance for successful implementation!

Driven by needs I have spent the past ten years facilitating the needs of groups. The important word here is *needs*. Why? Because groups, individuals, teams, committees, and, councils all have needs. Needs to contribute, needs to solve problems, needs to demonstrate a worthwhile reason for their existence within an organization or in society. Sometimes these needs are called goals or objectives or targets. And it's the facilitator who helps these groups and its individuals act in an expedient manner to fulfill these needs.

That is why facilitation is important.

You can make the difference Left to their own means, groups usually have a difficult time coming to closure on recommendations or action lists. That is why facilitation is important. So, here is an opportunity for you to make a positive difference in your business, church, council, club, or group. Your success depends on your mastery of the facilitation process. Shown below are some of the key elements required for successful facilitation.

Facilitation should help everyone commit to working together and getting results.

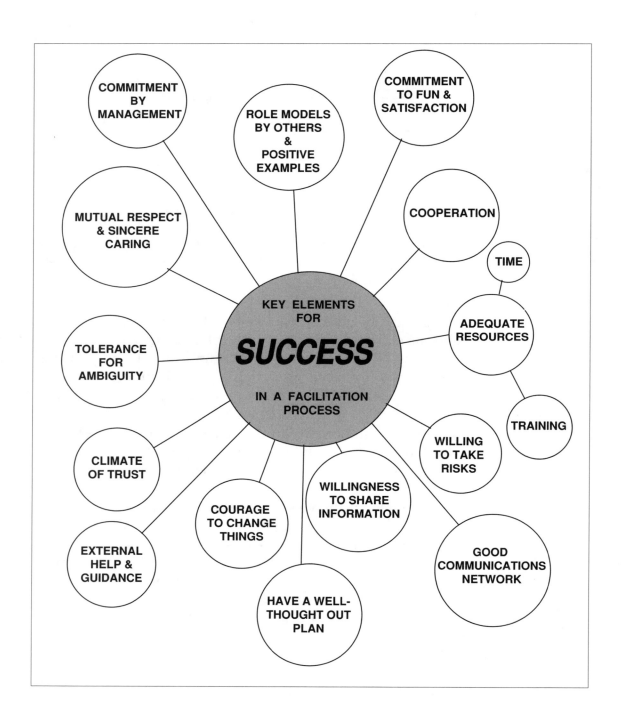

KEY ELEMENTS FOR
SUCCESS
IN A FACILITATION PROCESS

COMMITMENT BY MANAGEMENT
ROLE MODELS BY OTHERS & POSITIVE EXAMPLES
COMMITMENT TO FUN & SATISFACTION
MUTUAL RESPECT & SINCERE CARING
COOPERATION
TIME
ADEQUATE RESOURCES
TOLERANCE FOR AMBIGUITY
TRAINING
WILLING TO TAKE RISKS
CLIMATE OF TRUST
WILLINGNESS TO SHARE INFORMATION
COURAGE TO CHANGE THINGS
GOOD COMMUNICATIONS NETWORK
EXTERNAL HELP & GUIDANCE
HAVE A WELL-THOUGHT OUT PLAN

There are six steps to FACILITATION...

1 What is the **ISSUE** the group is trying to address?

2 What are the **CONCERNS** of each member of the group regarding this issue?

3 What are some **POSSIBILITIES** to solve the concerns?

4 What **CRITERIA** will the group use to judge each possibility?

5 What **ACTION** items will be selected from the list of possibilities?

6 **CHECK** to see if the action addresses the issue and the group's concerns.

1 Issue?

2 Concerns	3 Possibilities
5 Action	4 Criteria

6 Check?

The Bigger Picture

Six easy steps to success There are six steps in the facilitation process:

1. What's the **issue**?
2. What are your **concerns**?
3. What are some **possible solutions**?
4. Whare are our **criteria** for addressing this issue?
5. What are our **actions**?
6. Using a final **check**, do the actions address the issue?

Opening and closing spaces Keep in mind that these six steps are discrete activities managed by the facilitator. You will learn more about each of them in Section II, "Steps For Successful Facilitation." As you learn these steps, it is very helpful if you keep in mind the bigger picture of what this process does to achieve its ends. Each of the six steps takes the group through the process of opening and closing the common "spaces" used to solve problems.

ISSUE space
CONCERNS space
POSSIBILITIES space
CRITERIA space
SOLUTION (action) space
CHECKING space

The facilitator's role is to guide the group through these spaces. As the facilitator does this, the group's awareness level opens and closes. The following diagram illustrates this process.

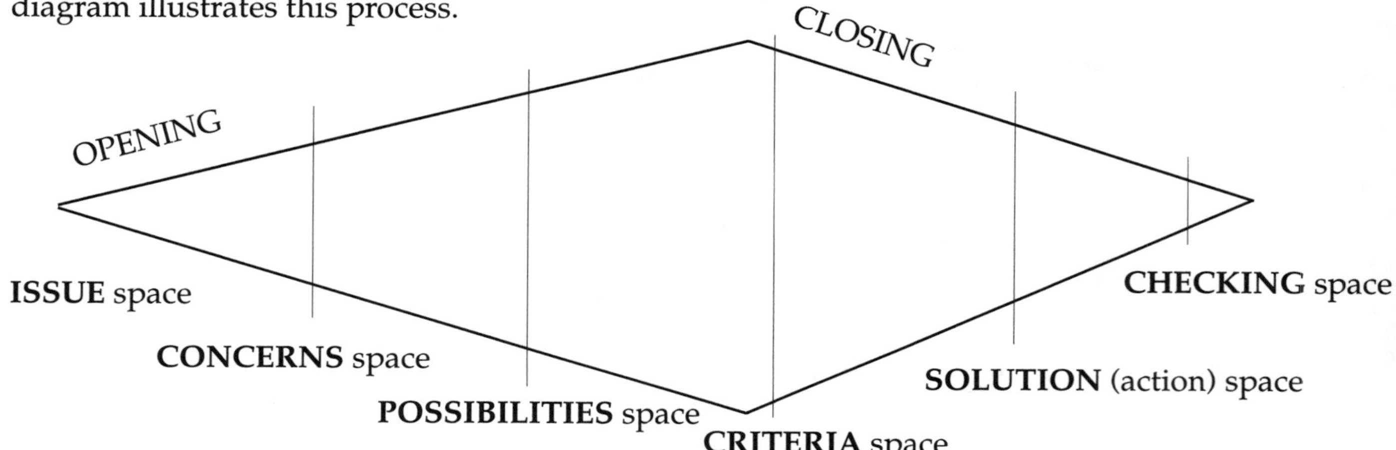

Alternatives to Facilitation

Ways to decide This six step facilitation process uses a rational, collaborative approach to solving problems. Groups can also make decisions is other ways:

- The person with the **highest rank** can decide
- The person with the **loudest voice** can decide
- Two or more participants can **force** their decision

Any of these three alternative methods might be justified depending on the situation surrounding the issue. As you will see, the collaborative approach is usually the best way to assure a wide base of support and successful implementation of the solution.

Other methods Listed below are alternative processes to collaborative facilitation. You will recognize each of them. Each has its value in solving problems and should be considered as the situation dictates.

BARGAINING This approach is similar to haggling and involves two parties in conflict over a single valuable "currency" (something of value to either party — for example, a benefit or a work rule). The process is not collaborative because it focuses on getting something at someone else's cost. It usually ends in some compromise where no one is 100% happy.

NEGOTIATION This approach is like bargaining but with multiple currencies. Many items are "on the table" and each party strives to maximize its winnings. Again, this is not a collaborative approach because each side focuses on winning its *position* and not addressing the root *interests or needs* of either party. The collaborative facilitation approach addresses interests and needs by using the concerns and possibilities steps.

MEDIATION This approach is a voluntary process where the parties agree to submit their disagreements to a third party (a mediator) for resolution. By definition, mediation is a nonbinding process and the mediator cannot impose any settlement on either party. A good mediator is like a referee and counselor combined into one person. It is not a collaborative process since neither party tries to benefit from the synergy of working together for a win-win solution and compromise is the end result.

ARBITRATION This approach is similar to mediation except that the results are binding. The arbitrator is empowered to decide an issue and award the winning party. The result of an arbitration is legally recognized in most states. It is not a collaborative process.

The best way Collaboration is the best way in nearly all situations. So, why don't we use it more often? The reason is the large amount of skill and effort required to do it correctly. A facilitated, collaborative problem-solving process requires dedication, time, and focus. But in the long run, it saves resources by eliminating rework.

> "It takes no skill to complain, but it takes a lot to participate in a collaborative process."

A collaborative problem solving process is one that allows people to work together in a productive manner to address issues. Consensus is the tool used for making decisions when you are collaborative. The end result of this process is a solution that all participants are willing to support (not necessarily agree with — but they will support it).

The most effective tool Facilitation is a way for any leader, manager, or president to assure things get done faster, thoroughly, and in a way that uses all the talents of the people involved. It is a superior approach to older methods of management fiat or unilateral decree. It is the most effective tool for modern organizations to fully utilize its human resource talents and create the inclusive work environment that is critical to high performance organizations.

Facilitation: easing, smoothing, speeding, expediting, quickening, hastening.

Collaboration

• Collaboration is an on-going process and not a one-shot event.

• Collaboration success is greatly enhanced by having a neutral, third-party facilitator.

• Collaboration requires that key decision makers are present and participate.

• Collaboration requires following the process and realizing that you must go slow to go fast.

• Collaboration is an open process and visible to anyone interested.

• Collaboration is an on-going education for its participants and requires participants to be knowledgeable about the issue.

• Collaboration requires the dedication of resources to make it work — human resources, time, money, and attention.

Some benefits of collaboration

1. It creates ownership in the solution
2. It increases the leadership skills of the participants
3. It produces more creative solutions by tapping group synergy
4. It builds confidence in taking risks

Facilitation IS and IS NOT

Facilitation IS

- A neutral process
- A balance between process and content
- Fair to everyone in the group
- Maximizing the involvement of everyone

Facilitation IS NOT

- Training
- Meeting management
- One-on-one coaching
- Group therapy

Benefits to participants

- More efficient use of time
- Clearer sense of progress towards a goal
- Increased opportunity to participate
- Greater post-session support for decisions or recommendations
- Increased leadership skills

Examples of facilitation applications

- Incident investigations
- Customer service teams
- Cross-functional planning groups
- Problem-solving teams
- Ad hoc committees
- Contract resolution teams

> Facilitation helps reveal the "buried treasure" that every person brings to the group.

Review

The Facilitation Process

- Collaborative problem solving is best
- There are six steps in the facilitation process
- The process must have adequate resources dedicated to it
- A neutral facilitator is critical to the success of the process
- Other non-collaborative processes also exist for facilitator's use

And remember...

• It's always easier to complain than it is to tackle the problem using a collaborative approach!

• High performance organizations use team problem-solving and neutral facilitation to create inclusive work environments.

• Facilitation is not the same as training — facilitation does more. Training enables individuals to develop specific skills while facilitation also provides closure by a group, in the form of some output, from a problem-solving process.

"We are all inclined to judge ourselves by our ideals, others by their acts."
— **Harold Nicholson**

> "Pull the string, and it will follow you wherever you wish. Push it, and it will go nowhere at all.
> **— Dwight D. Eisenhower**

2 YOUR JOB AS FACILITATOR

A facilitator is neutral

Why a facilitator? To *facilitate* is to make the accomplishment of some task easy or easier. Facilitation is a process of making human interactions easier and more effective in attaining a goal or objective. The *facilitator* helps the group succeed.

Critical roles A facilitator is a neutral servant of the group. He or she focuses the energy of the group towards a common goal and keeps the group moving towards that goal. The facilitator's job also includes pre-meeting logistics and handling paperwork afterwards.

The facilitator owns the process and the group owns the content. Accordingly, the facilitator makes suggestions and judgments and takes action in regard to the procedures and sequencing of group events (the process). He or she does not evaluate ideas (the content) of the group. In all cases, the facilitator protects individuals from attack to assure that the playing field is level and everyone has an equal opportunity to participate. This role of "protector" is essential to stimulating participation and maintaining trust in the room. Finally, the facilitator has to stay at least one step ahead of the group.

We'll look closer at these responsibilities in this chapter.

A Facilitator is...

Facilitator helps the group and remains neutral

- **Enthusiastic** about causing positive change through team action!
- A **salesperson** for the concept of team problem-solving!
- A **role model** and **mentor** for others in the area of facilitation and team problem-solving!
- **Brave** and not afraid of groups!
- **Willing to help others** solve their problems!

The facilitator owns the process.

The group owns the content.

The organization owns the results.

The organization also owns the responsibility to provide the facilitator and the group all the support necessary to make them a success. Any less would be a tragedy — a waste of human resources, money, and trust.

And to be a success, there are three fundamental requirements that everyone shares responsibility for:

Everyone's Responsibility

- The group must have a **clear purpose**.
- The participants must be **committed** to the purpose, to the process, and to the belief that they will have some benefit from, or stake in, the outcome.
- The process must be given **adequate resources** (time, money, human resources, support) for its successful completion.

Balancing PUSHING and PULLING the group

When you facilitate, you have to balance pushing and pulling of the group.

What is pushing? Every time the facilitator makes a proposal to the group, that's a push. Every time the facilitator takes sides or shows favoritism, that's a push. When you make a change in the process, that's a push.

Is pushing bad? Pushing is not necessarily bad. When you push a group you will experience varying degrees of push-back or resistance. Resistance can be in two forms: passive or aggressive. Passive resistance is a problem and causes difficulties because of its undetectable nature - it is like a volcano awaiting to erupt. On the other hand, active resistance is good because it is open and can be dealt with.

Is it OK to push? There will be times during the facilitation process that you'll need to make a change or introduce something new. Pushing a group is therefore acceptable. But here's the important lesson to remember: *once you have pushed, stop and pull.*

What's a pull? A pull involves creating a void. You do this by asking sincere questions, such as "We have come to an impasse, what would the group like to do now?" or "I sense that the group is tired, what should our next step be?" Another push is silence. Any action by the facilitator that creates a vacuum or void is a way to pull the group. Try it. You'll find that pulling a group is an effective, powerful way to lead the process.

1. Stay neutral
2. Balance your pushes and pulls
3. Protect all participants from attack
4. Enforce the rules

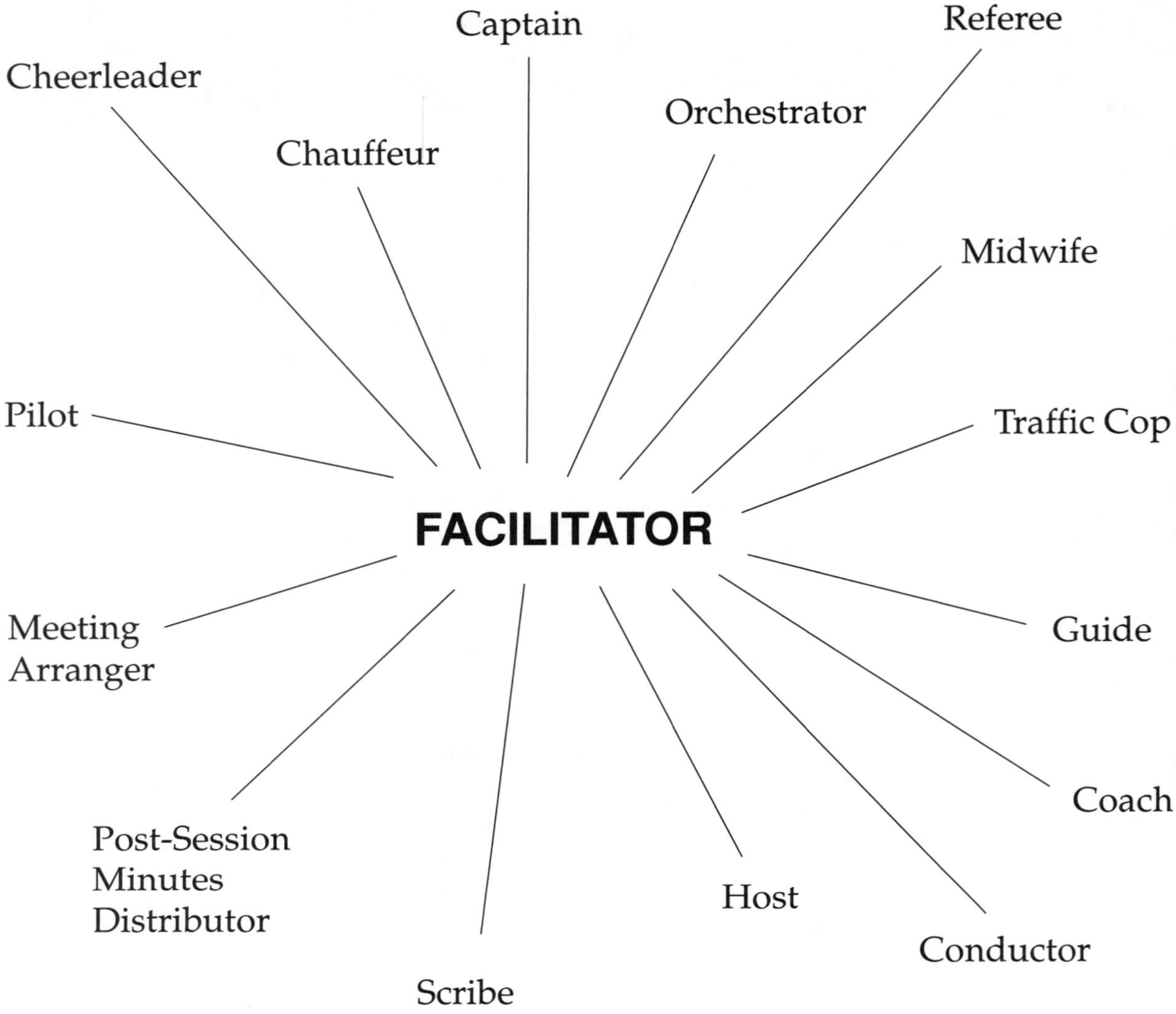

Captain

Referee

Cheerleader

Orchestrator

Chauffeur

Midwife

Pilot

Traffic Cop

FACILITATOR

Meeting
Arranger

Guide

Coach

Post-Session
Minutes
Distributor

Host

Conductor

Scribe

The facilitator has many jobs!

DESIRED BEHAVIORS

A successful facilitator exhibits certain attributes and behaviors. Listed below are important ones you should keep in mind.

Do not evaluate It is tempting to make positive or negative remarks, no matter how subtle, when a participant offers an idea or concern. A common error is saying, "Good idea" or "That's good" after receiving a comment. That might seem harmless is saying but it sends a message of approval that is not in-line with being neutral. Instead, simply say, "Thank you."

Encourage participation Be proactive in seeking input, as well as confronting problem behaviors that discourage participation.

Be positive A facilitator's enthusiasm is contagious. Stay upbeat and positive — regardless of the situation. Your positive attitude is important and serves as a good role model for the participants. Becoming upset or negative will not help any situation. Remember that you are the group's guide during troubled times in the process.

Stay neutral Just as a facilitator cannot evaluate participants' ideas, a facilitator cannot take sides. Staying neutral means showing complete impartiality during the process. Especially be wary of subtle messages you could mistakenly send the group, such as comments like, "I think management will go for that idea" or "Is that really what you want to say with the current organization setup?" Again, a simple "Thank you" is always the best acknowledgment.

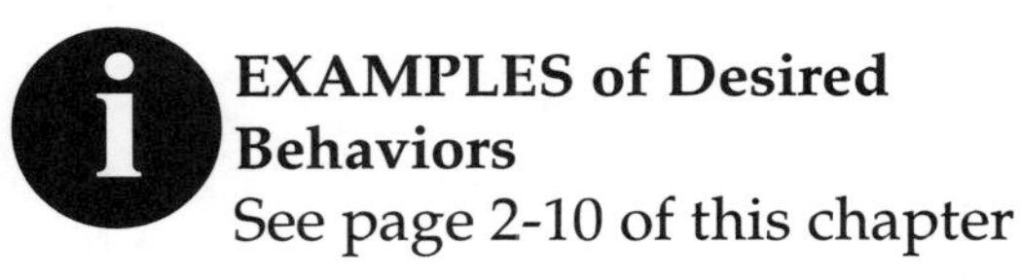
EXAMPLES of Desired Behaviors
See page 2-10 of this chapter

Educate the group As guide and owner of the process, you have the responsibility to teach the group in the steps and methods necessary for successful completion of the facilitation. It is entirely permissible to say, "Time out. Let me show you how to proceed in this step."

GROUP OWNS IT

CONTENT

WHAT the group has to accomplish...

- Agenda
- Issue
- Job
- Decisions
- Action Items
- Plans
- Assignments

YOU OWN IT

PROCESS

HOW the group works together...

- Involvement
- Trust
- Openness
- Pace
- Equality
- Sequence of tasks
- Checks & Validations

ETHICAL ISSUES

How could this happen? Facilitators occasionally fall into ethical dilemmas while facilitating. The far most common problem involves being neutral. This usually arises from a conflict between the facilitator's interest and the group's interest. Whether it is perceived or real, such conflict seriously damages the facilitators effectiveness. If this situation occurs, the facilitator should immediately excuse herself or himself and inform the leader.

Other Examples Aside from not being neutral, three other ethical problems could arise during the facilitation process. The first would be inconsistencies or incompatibilities between the personal values of the facilitator and the goals and/or strategies of the group (for example, the group proposes to do an illegal or immoral act) A second possibility would be some unforeseen consequence of an intervention by the facilitator that is incompatible with the facilitator's personal values (for example, as a result of the facilitator's intervening in a personal conflict within the group, one of the parties is later assaulted and injured). A third, and less drastic dilemma, is when the skill level of the facilitator is below the requirements to deal with the complexity of the issue.

What to do? In all cases, the facilitator must cease being the group's facilitator. There should be no hesitation or attempt to sway the group in favor of the facilitator. Tell the leader and gracefully bow out. Period.

TRIP WIRES

The following situations will cause you problems while facilitating. Watch out for them!

- Being a "nay-sayer"
- Railroading decisions
- Judging the worth of ideas or comments
- Failing to use positive reinforcement
- Being continually inaccurate when recording ideas
- Dominating the discussion
- Insensitive to the needs of participants
- Neglecting to make the group accountable for its actions
- Having an incomplete or unrealistic agenda

OTHER CHALLENGES

Here are some more challenges for the facilitator:

- Confusion about the roles and authority of the group
- Time pressures
- Resistance to change
- Low level of patience — either group or facilitator
- Multiple issues are present in the session
- Group has a low tolerance for ambiguity
- Lack of facilitation skills and/or experience
- Group preoccupation with "jumping to the solution"

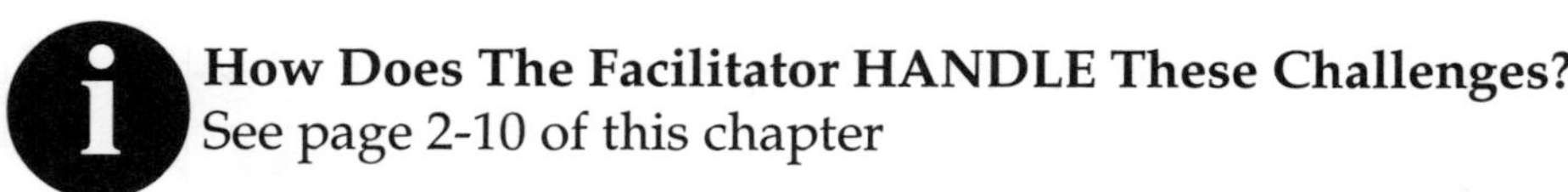

How Does The Facilitator HANDLE These Challenges?
See page 2-10 of this chapter

A POSITIVE CLIMATE

Here are some characteristics of a positive climate. Look for these in your facilitation sessions.

- Everyone's contributions are valued
- Collaboration is high
- Competition is low
- Participants laugh aloud — and often
- Participants are interested in the issue
- Discussion are open and honest and friendly

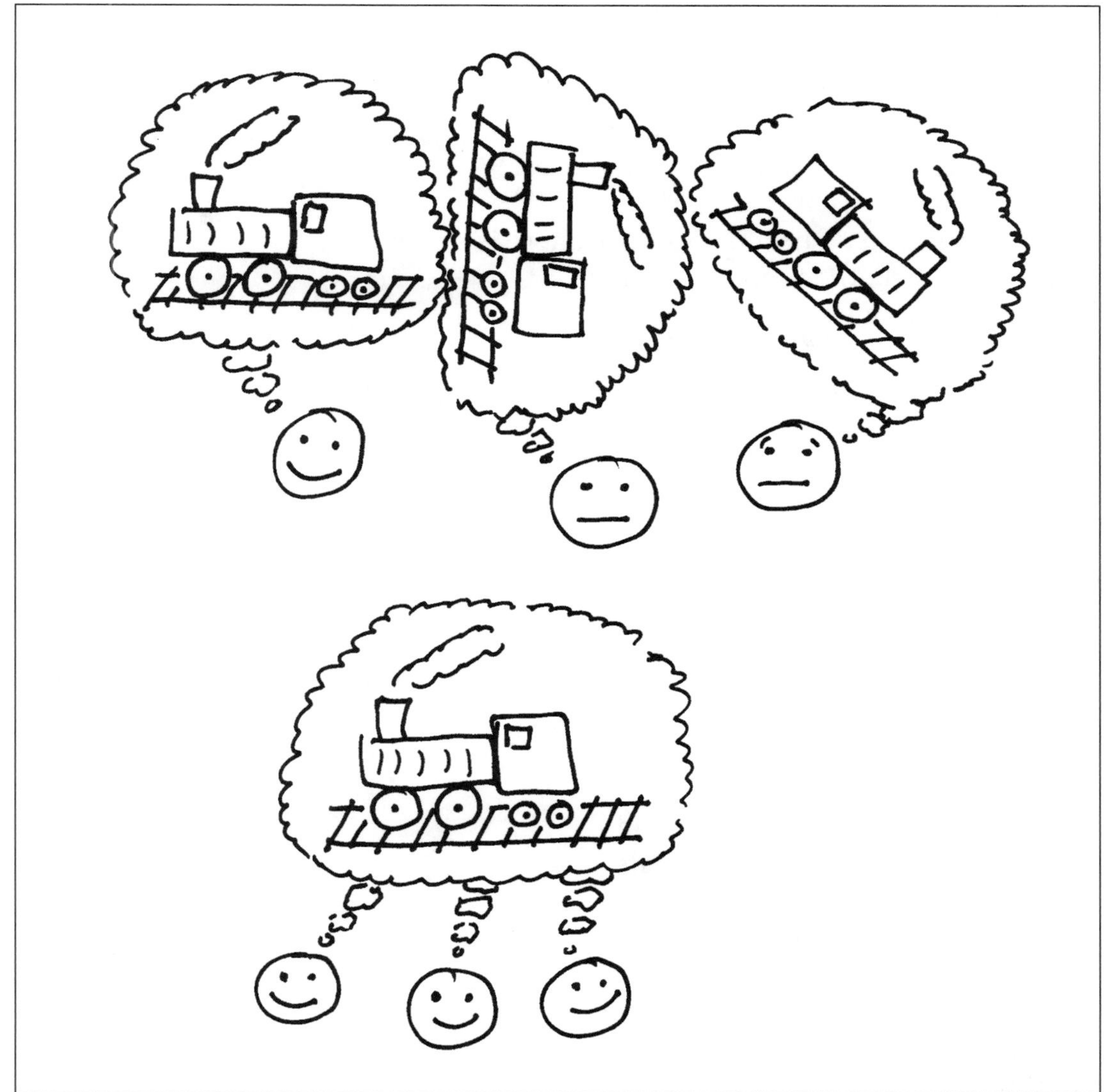

Make sure that everyone in the room is on the same track.

A Little Humor...

20 Things A Facilitator DOES NOT Say

1. "Does your train of thought have a caboose?"
2. "I don't know what your problem is, but I'll bet it's hard to pronounce."
3. "I see you've set aside this special time to humiliate yourself in public."
4. "I'm really easy to get along with once you people learn to worship me."
5. "I'll try being nicer if you try being smarter!"
6. "It sounds like English but I can't understand a word you're saying!"
7. "I like you. You remind me of when I was young and stupid."
8. "Thank you. We're all refreshed and challenged by your unique point of view."
9. "I'm not being rude. You're just insignificant."
10. "Do I look like a people person?"
11. "You have a PBS mind in a MTV world!"
12. "I'm trying to image you with a personality."
13. "Can I trade this job for what's behind Door Number One?"
14. "Too many freaks and not enough circuses!"
15. "Nice aftershave. Must you marinate in it?"
16. "Chaos, panic and disorder... my work here is done!"
17. "If I throw a stick, then will you leave?"
18. "Sarcasm is just one more service I offer."
19. "You! Off our planet!!"
20. "Whatever point you were trying to make... you missed!"

A Little Advice...

10 Things A Facilitator DOES

1. Show enthusiasm for ideas
2. Remain as neutral as possible
3. Move around the room while talking
4. Be patient and never angry or hostile
5. Remain open-minded and accepting
6. Be open to receiving feedback — and giving it
7. Be an active listener
8. Watch for early warning signs of tension and disruption
9. Discuss the tough issues when necessary
10. Ask useful and though-provoking questions

Review

The Facilitator

- Owns the process
- Acts as a resource, not a policeman
- Is neutral
- Explains the six-step process
- Balances pushing and pulling

And remember...

- The group is responsible for the content.
- The facilitator is a role model and exhibits the desired behaviors.
- The facilitator has many roles.
- Humor is the facilitator's best friend.

"It's easier for people to see it your way, if you first see it their way."
— **Jack Kaine**

> "When I assume, I make an ass out of u and me."
> — **Chuck Pendley**, *Operations & Supervisor Trainer*

3 THE ROLE OF THE PARTICIPANTS

Don't assume In a book designed for helping facilitators, why do we discuss the role of participants? We often assume that everyone knows how to be "good" participant in a problem-solving group. We also assume that each person in the room instinctively knows how to behave and contribute to the process.

Bad things can happen Having these assumptions is a mistake. And these assumptions commonly lead to misunderstandings within a group that can escalate io mistrust and counterproductive (bad) behaviors by participants.

Two roles So, let's look at the role of participants. By understanding their role in this process, you'll be able to (1) explain it to them, and (2) reinforce the desired behaviors when you see them. There are two types of roles for participants: task roles and process roles. You'll learn more about them in this chapter.

Facilitator
Leader
Participant

Task Roles

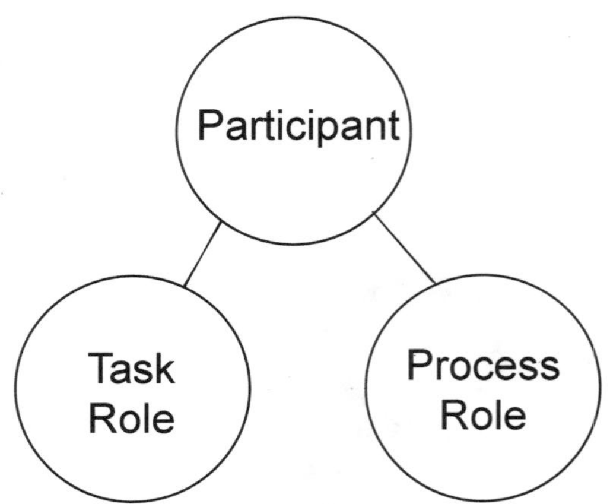

Benefits of task roles Having task roles improves a group's performance. First, having participants perform certain jobs helps the facilitator by eliminating time-consuming tasks. As a result, the facilitator can focus more on the process and less on clerical details. Second, having task roles for the participants creates a sense of inclusiveness and ownership in the process. This elevated level of participation intensifies the feeling ownership by the group.

Different task roles This type of role is function-oriented. It involves the performance of specific tasks by the participant. Examples are:

- Time Keeper
- Recorder
- Flipchart Hanger
- Logistics Manager

Not every group member will have a task role. There are usually more participants in a group than jobs. Each participant does, however, have a process role to fulfill.

Other roles There are other roles besides the task roles and process roles of participants in a problem-solving process. Fundamentally, there are three types of individuals in this type of process: the participant, the leader, and the facilitator. This chapter exclusively deals with the roles of the participant. However, there is another special class of participant (or pseudo-participant) that you should be aware of — the stakeholder. This special participant is not always in the room during the session but has vast influence over the success of the group.

You will learn more about the stakeholder in Chapter 10, "Getting Started." You can also learn more about the role of the leader in Chapter 11, "You And The Leader."

Task Roles

Time Keeper

• Gets time deadlines for each process step from facilitator
• Announces warnings
"15 minutes"
"5 minutes"
"1 minute"

BENEFIT: Keeps group on schedule & finishes on time.

INCREASES OWNERSHIP

Recorder

• Assists facilitator (as a scribe) to write information on flipcharts

BENEFIT: Allows facilitator to focus on process and group participation.

INCREASES OWNERSHIP

TASK ROLES

Flipchart Hanger

• Assists recorder and facilitator by hanging flipcharts on the wall

BENEFIT: Allows the recorder to keep writing without interruption.

INCREASES OWNERSHIP

Logistics Manager

• Sets up room
• Arranges for meals and snacks
• Sends out reminders for follow-up meetings
• Schedules room for future meetings

BENEFIT: Frees the facilitator from this drudgery.

INCREASES OWNERSHIP

Process Roles

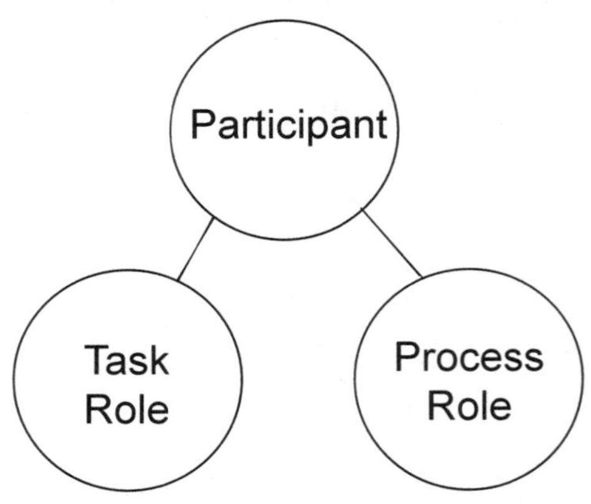

Process roles This type of role is very different from the task role. It requires each group member to actively participate in the process. Process roles are the core behaviors required for a successful problem solving session. These roles are:

- **Listen to others**
  Be an active listener. Always first seek to understand others in the group.
- **Make commitments**
  Be decisive and willing to vocally express your commitment to group actions and decisions.
- **Initiate activity**
  Be proactive. Anticipate group needs and be the first to suggest and take action. Don't always wait for someone else in the group to do something... YOU do it!
- **Seek information**
  Be inquisitive. Avoid assumptions and never hesitate to ask questions when unsure about something.
- **Relieve tension**
  Be an agent for humor and lightheartedness in the group. Be positive. Be upbeat. Be a role model for others by projecting a positive attitude and seeking to defuse tense situations.
- **Obey groundrules**
  Be an ally to the facilitator. Obey the group's groundrules and help enforce them when others break them.
- **Test for consensus**
  At the appropriate time during the process, ask the group if there is consensus. Help the facilitator by asking this question. Be vigilant in openly seeking group support and buy-in for positions and actions.
- **Help others**
  Watch for others needing help... offer help and don't wait for it to be asked.
- **Share concerns**
  Have the courage to share your feelings and thoughts before the group. Be a role model for others.
- **Help the facilitator**
  Someday you'll have to be a facilitator and you'll understand how important this behavior is. Alert the facilitator if she or he stops being neutral. Suggest ways to improve the process. Offer to scribe or hang flipcharts. Provide feedback to the facilitator afterwards regarding ways to improve the process or the session.
- **Contribute ideas**
  You are present in the group to contribute. You are already contributing your time so why not also contribute your talent and experience? You CAN make the difference!

Facilitator's responsibility
The facilitator must clearly explain these process roles at the beginning of the first session. Allow 15 to 30 minutes at the start of it to review all the roles — the facilitator's role, the participants' roles, and the roles of any others (leader, stakeholder, etc.).

Process Roles

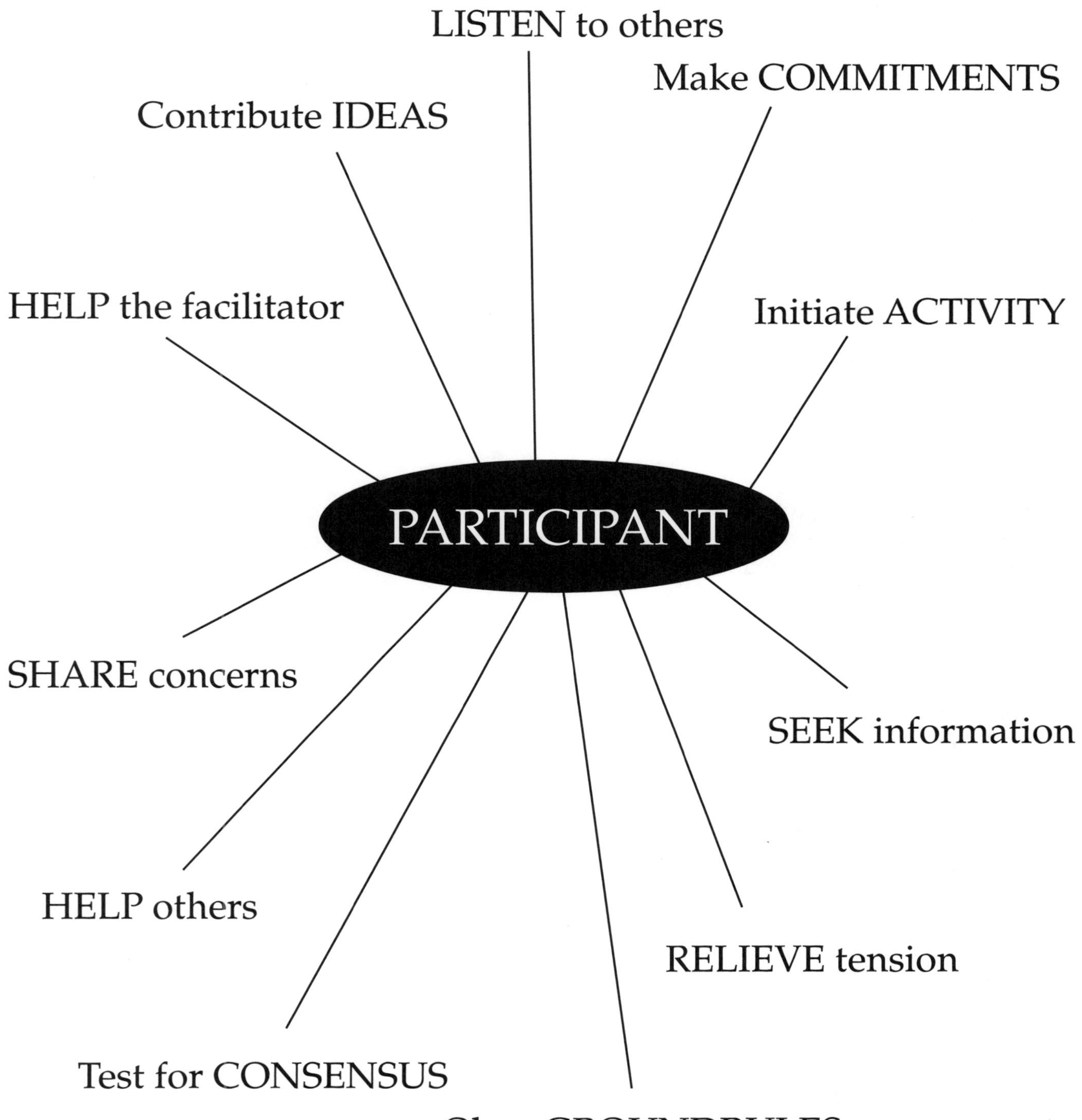
LISTEN to others
Make COMMITMENTS
Contribute IDEAS
HELP the facilitator
Initiate ACTIVITY
PARTICIPANT
SHARE concerns
SEEK information
HELP others
RELIEVE tension
Test for CONSENSUS
Obey GROUNDRULES

Lessons From The Geese

A Story To Help Participants Understand Their Role

Animal research shows geese behave as very effective groups. When flying in formation, each bird flaps its wings and creates uplift for the bird immediately following. By flying in such a "V" formation, the whole flock adds at least 71% greater flying range than if each bird flew on its own.

Lesson:
People who are part of a team and share a common destination can get where they are going quicker and more easily because they are traveling on the trust of one another.

Whenever a goose falls out formation, it suddenly feels the drag and resistance of trying to go it alone and quickly gets back into formation to take advantage of the power of the flock.

Lesson:
If we have as much sense as a goose, we will share information with those who are headed the same way we are going.

When the lead goose tires, he rotates back in the wing and another goose takes over. Without a thought, the lead goose turns over leadership of the group who has fresh energy.

Lesson:
It pays to share leadership and take turns doing hard jobs. Gamesmanship and egos get in the way of sharing leadership, recognizing fresh ideas, and keeping up group momentum. Putting individual egos aside contributes to team progress.

(continued)

The geese honk from behind to encourage those up front to keep up their speed.

Lesson:
Words of support and inspiration help energize those on the front line and help them keep pace in spite of the day-to-day pressures and fatigue.

When a goose gets sick or is wounded by a gunshot and falls out of formation, two more geese fall out of the formation and follow the injured one down to help and protect him. They stay with him until he is either able to fly or until he is dead. And then, they launch out with another formation to catch up with their group.

Lesson:
If we have the sense of a goose, we will stand by each other when things get rough.

Finally, relying on their group instincts, the signals and wisdom of individual members of the flock, the flock modifies its course when they sense an adverse condition ahead of them. Thus, the flock plans for changes that may affect them adversely, rather that reacting to those changes which come up unexpectedly. Their combined instincts, loyalty and lack of ego keep the group in tact, because survival is the goal which drives their actions. They are a hardy group, as witnessed by their vast population increase despite some very real threats to their survival.

The next time you see a formation of geese, remember…

As a member of a team, your chances for survival and prosperity are vastly increased. It is a reward, a challenge, and a privilege to be a contributing member of a team!

Participants' Credo

I am involved.
I ask questions.
I collaborate.
I ask for help when confused.
I am open, brave and honest.
I respect others.
I listen.
I care.

Q & A

Question

Can a person effectively be both a participant (process role) and, say, a recorder (task role)?

Answer

Yes. And the facilitator must actively include the task-role person in the process. For example, the facilitator must repeatedly ask the recorder, "What are your ideas?"

Question

Can there be "role overlap" between task roles?

Answer

Yes.

Question

I've heard the term "scribe" used also. What's the difference between a scribe and a recorder?

Answer

In the strictest sense, a scribe records information on a flipchart and a recorder takes notes that are refined into group meeting minutes. In this book, the terms will be used interchangeably and mean someone who records thoughts and ideas on a flipchart.

Review

Participants' Roles

1. Participant roles must be clearly explained to group by the facilitator.

2. Each participant has a process role. Some (not all) group members have a task role.

3. Process roles are:
    > listen to others
    > make commitments
    > initiate activity
    > seek information
    > relieve tension
    > obey groundrules
    > test for consensus
    > help others
    > shares concerns
    > helps the facilitator
    > contributes ideas

4. Task roles are:
    + Time Keeper
    + Recorder
    + Flipchart Hanger
    + Logistics Manager

And remember...

• Geese work together towards a common goal by each taking a defined role. Work groups can have the same success by doing the same!

"Assumption is the mother of mistake."
— **Unknown**

1 Issue?

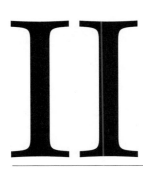

2 Concerns	3 Possibilities
5 Action	4 Criteria

6 Check?

II

Steps For Successful Facilitation

4. What's The **Issue**?
5. What Are Our **Concerns**?
6. Any Possible **Solutions**?
7. Our **Criteria**?
8. What's Our **Action**?
9. **Check**?

"We evolve, not by dreaming of giant steps, but by committing ourselves in action to little ones, moving step by relentless step to an ever-expanding field of vision."

— **Nathaniel Branden**

> "It isn't that they can't see the solution. It is that they can't see the problem."
>
> — **G.K. Chesterton**

4 ISSUE?

What's the issue? How often we forget to ask!

Committees, teams, and groups typically form to address some problem, concern, or issue. That's not uncommon. What is troublesome, however, is that if no one asks the obvious question "Why are we here?" at the meeting's start it could become embarrassing later... or worse!

As a facilitator, assume that nothing is a "given" or common knowledge to all the participants. A quick poll of people in the room can quickly sort out any differences of opinion over the purpose or subject of the session.

If differences arise, then work with the group to agree on what single issue they would like to address at today's session. Major topics that fall outside that issue can be recorded on an "Issues Bin" sheet on the room wall and addressed at another meeting.

If the group cannot agree on the issue, then stop and adjourn. At that point, consult the leader for direction and reschedule another meeting.

1 Issue?

2 Concerns	3 Possibilities
5 Action	4 Criteria

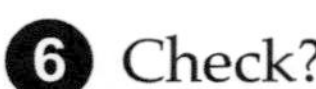
6 Check?

WHAT'S THE ISSUE?

1. **Ask the group, "What's the issue?"** Go around the room and have each person give his or her idea of today's issue.

2. **Write down each person's comment**. Use a flipchart so everyone can see.

3. **Find any common elements of the ideas written on the flipchart.** Circle identical words or phrases. Have the group help you.

4. **Build a draft issue statement.** Use a clean flipchart sheet. Look at the circled words and phrases on the other flipchart. Using these common ideas, write a draft issue. *Warning: Avoid the trap of writing a solution statement instead of an issue statement.*

5. **Have the group help you revise the draft statement.** Cross out words. Add words. Rearrange words. It's OK to end up with a messy flipchart but make sure that the groups helps you make the changes!

6. **Ask the group, "Is this the issue?"** Have them look at the revised issue statement you've written on the flipchart. Allow plenty of time for everyone to think about it. Make any suggested changes to your draft issue statement.

7. **Get the group to agree.** One last time, ask the group if they can all support the issue as written on the flipchart. If not, find out what has to be changed to get everyone to support the issue. Then ask again, "Is this the issue?" and look at each person in the room, making eye contact, to make sure that each and every person agrees.

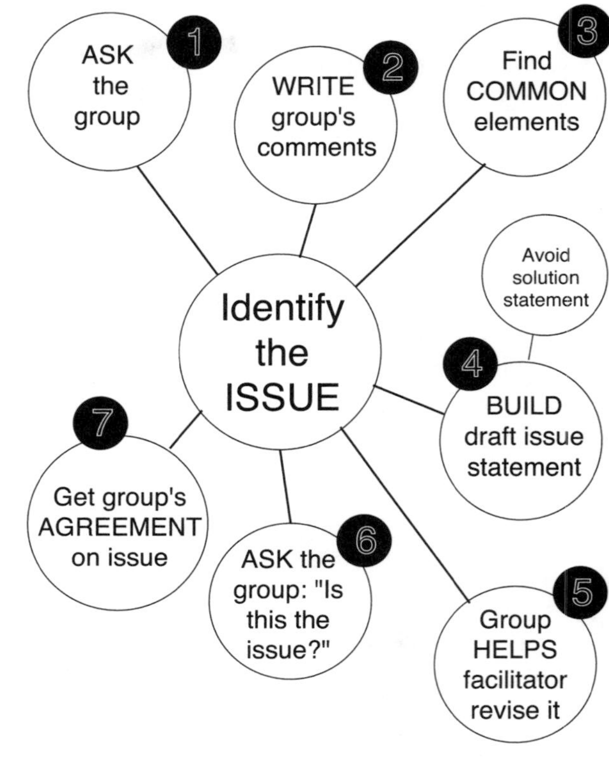

HINT: Sometimes the group identifies more than one valid issue! Fortunately, you can facilitate the group in only <u>one</u> issue at a time. So, the other valid issues should be listed on a separate flipchart titled *"Other Issues To Be Worked In Future."* By validating the existence of other issues and identifying them for future facilitation sessions, you help the group move ahead by avoiding those unproductive group arguments over "that's not a issue — yes it's an issue!"

Case Study: What's the Issue?

Background
The random drug testing team had their first meeting on Tuesday. During this two hour session, Tom, the facilitator, reviewed the management's instructions to the team, discussed the key stakeholders, and gathered everyone's *concerns*.

The team met for three more meetings during the following weeks. Tom had the group brainstorm *possibilities* and agree on a list of *criteria*. During the fifth meeting, the random drug testing team developed specific *action items* (in the form of recommendations to management) using their lists of possibilities and criteria.

Half way through this fifth session Tom had to adjourn the group early because it became polarized over the wording of the recommendations. Half the group wanted to recommend punishment for those employees failing to take or pass the Company's random drug tests. The balance wanted to recommend steps in the procedure of administering random drug testing at the plant and not address nature of any punishment. Each side argued for the validity of their recommendations.

The Problem
Tom saw that this team was deadlocked. Neither faction would acknowledge the recommendations of the other. After five meetings the team was nowhere near consensus on any output. What had happened?

It is clear that the team was not clear on the issue. A common error, everyone assumed that everyone else held the same definition of the issue. Tom did not take the time initially to review the issue with the group. He assumed that everyone knew the "random drug testing" meant "creating a plant policy on conducting random drug testing." After all, that was the instruction given to him from the management team.

What Happened?
Tom had assumed wrong.

At the sixth meeting Tom polled the membership and was surprised at the variety of responses to his question, "What do you think the issue is?"

Yvette said, "The issue is 'Making sure everyone complies with the new random drug testing program'."

Eddy said, "Keeping our plant drug free!"

Jack said, "Getting employees to live healthier by avoiding drugs and alcohol."

Tom, as facilitator, should have made the team agree at the first meeting on the issue. Once they agreed on a single issue future disagreements would have been avoided.

The Lesson
Do these steps at your *first meeting*:

1. Poll the room asking, "What do you think the issue is?"
2. Write each response on a flipchart.
3. Rewrite the responses into a single Issue Statement.
4. Get the group's consensus (edit the Issue Statement as required).
5. Post the Issue Statement on the wall.
6. Refer back to the Issue Statement throughout the facilitation process.

> **Warning**: Define the issue in terms of needs, not solutions.

ISSUE

OUR ISSUE IS:

Creating a plant policy on conducting random drug testing.

Alice Meets The Cheshire Cat

The Cat only grinned when it saw Alice. It looked good-natured, she thought: still it had very long claws and a great many teeth, so she felt that it ought to be treated with respect.

"Cheshire Puss," she began, rather timidly, as she did not at all know whether it would like the name: however, it only grinned a little wider. "Come, it's pleased do far," thought Alice, and she went on.

"Would you tell me, please, which way I ought to go from here?"

"That depends a good deal on where you want to get to," said the Cat.

"I don't much care where —," said Alice.

"Then it doesn't matter which way you go," said the Cat.

" — so long as I get somewhere," said Alice.

"Oh, you're sure to do that," said the Cat, "if only you walk long enough."

--- Lewis Carroll, 1865

The Lesson - Without a clear issue statement, groups end up moving ahead but really get nowhere after all the work is finished.

Issue Statements

Not an action statement One problem frequently encountered by facilitators is an issue statement written as a solution. It is tempting for a group to word the issue as solution, such as "Construct new cafeteria" instead of the proper issue statement "Quality of plant food." It is the facilitator's job to notice this mistake and rewrite the statement.

Write and rewrite Developing consensus on the issue is easy done using a blank flipchart sheet. The first step involving polling each participant on his or her interpretation of the issue and recording their response on the flipchart. Then circle the key words and write a draft statement. Then write and rewrite until everyone agrees with the issue statement on the flipchart.

Plain sight in the room After the group agrees on the issue state, it is important to display it every session. The easiest way to do this is posting a flipchart sheet with the issue written on it. This allows both the participants and the facilitator to refer to poster if any question arises regarding whether the discussion addresses the issue.

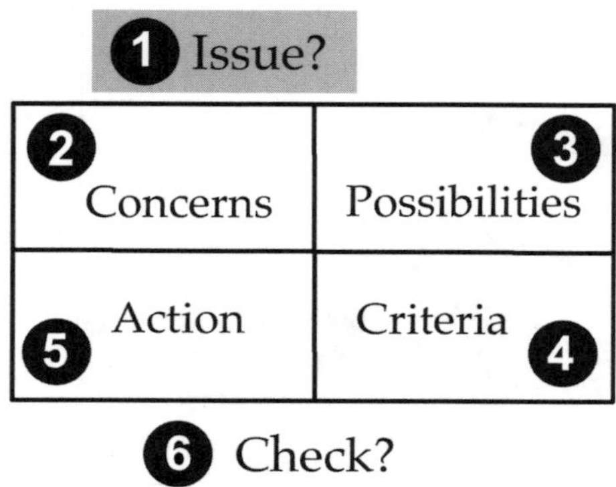

Review

Issue?

• Always identify the issue being addressed. Too often, a facilitator assumes everyone knows the issue and the group tries to solve the problem without first understanding it. This mistake soon causes delays and back-tracking.

• In the beginning, ask each participant what he or she thinks the issue is. Then proceed to build a commonly understood and accepted issue statement on a flipchart sheet.

• Always post the issue statement on the wall of the meeting room.

And remember...

• Without a clear, written issue statement it is difficult to proceed with the facilitation process. Please do not consider this step a formality that can be skipped. It provides everyone in the room an opportunity to fully understand and support the topic being addressed. Without a clear understanding of the issue, groups can lose valuable time later by having to redo the concerns and possibilities.

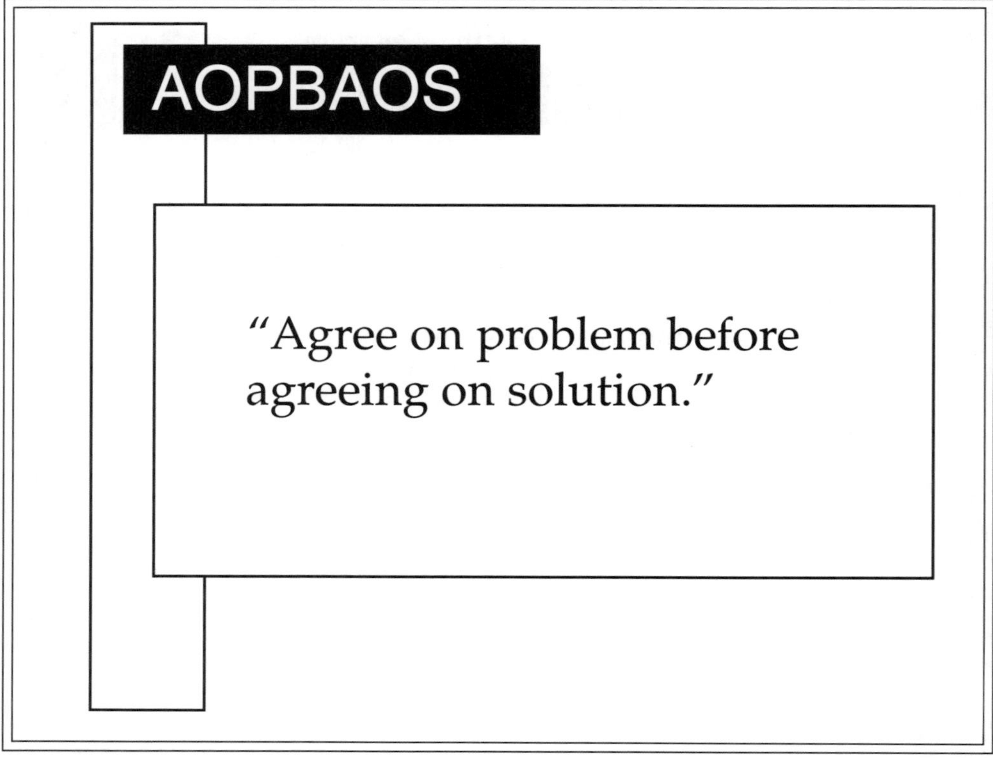
AOPBAOS
"Agree on problem before agreeing on solution."

> "They call him 'Jigsaw' because every time he's faced with a problem, he goes to pieces."
>
> — **Anon.**

CONCERNS?

How do you **feel** about this issue?

What are you **concerned** about? What do you **think** about this issue?

Gathering the concerns of each individual in the group is very important. It provides each person an opportunity to explore his or her feelings about the issue at hand.

There is no judgement of anyone's thoughts and feelings during this step in the process. You as the facilitator need to be active in discouraging comments and discussions.

All concerns should be recorded on a flipchart and hung on the walls of the meeting room. They will be used later in Step 6 when the team checks its action items to assure that they address the issue... and the concerns of the group.

Gathering concerns is an important step in facilitation process for two reasons. First, it forces each member of the group to focus on the issue. And second, it provides a helpful reference during the brainstorming of solutions.

1 Issue?

2 Concerns	3 Possibilities
5 Action	4 Criteria

6 Check?

Guidelines for gathering concerns

• Concerns are the thoughts, feelings, reflections, and impressions of each member of the group. *They are not how someone else feels or thinks about the issue.* Concerns are personal.

• Concerns always begin with "I think..." or "I feel..." or "I'm concerned about..."

• There should be no debate, no criticism, nor any challenges to a person's concern. Period.

• Start off by offering an example. Then ask for a volunteer for the first concern. Go around the room asking each member for one concern... keep going until the group is finished.

• Don't put anyone in an awkward situation... just tell them "It's OK if you'd like to pass on this round."

• After you write a person's concern on the flipchart sheet, ask them to read it and then ask, "Is this what you mean?"

• Post the flipchart sheets because you'll need them in Step Three during the brainstorming of possibilities.

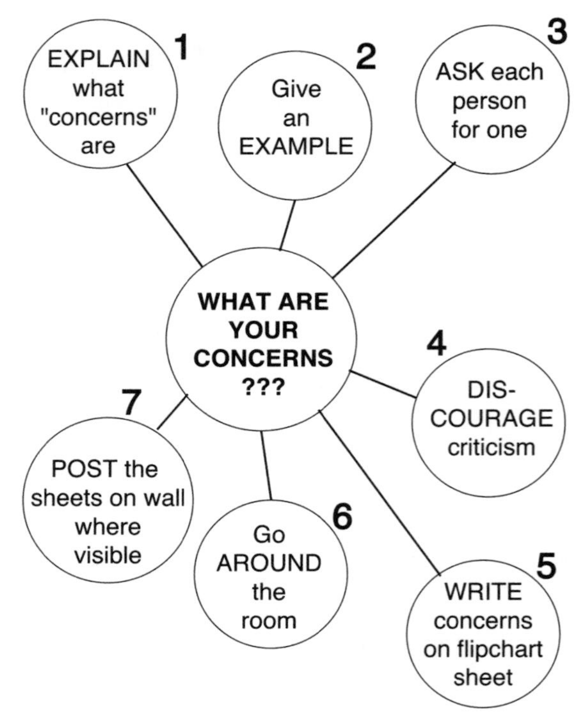

1 Issue?

2 Concerns	3 Possibilities
5 Action	4 Criteria

6 Check?

Case Study: What are your concerns?

Background

Will was quiet most of the time. Dedicated to his routine duties, Will worked in the Purchasing Department as a clerk for the past eight years. He was cooperative with fellow workers but was not a person to speak his mind in public.

Judy, his supervisor, had called a meeting today to resolve a long-standing problem within the group: errors in entering data into the department's shipping records. She was concerned that both the shipping and receiving clerks were being careless. Despite her coaching of individuals on the correct procedures, many errors were still being made.

Tom, the facilitator, began the meeting in the usual way. He announced to the group his role as a neutral facilitator and reviewed the process that they would follow. After the group agreed on their boundaries, rules, and stakeholders, Tom reviewed the issue with them and obtained the group's consensus on the issue statement.

Tom next gathered concerns from the group. Before starting, he reiterated that *concerns were the thoughts, feelings, reflections, and impressions* of each person in the room regarding the issue. There is no right or wrong concern and, so, no criticism permitted during this step of the process.

Tom started with the first person on his right. Tara, a shipping clerk, boldly said, "I'm concerned that no matter what we do, it'll never be good enough for management." The next person in the circle, Josh, said, "I think that our computer equipment and software is outdated and isn't the right stuff to have!"

After collecting the concerns of several more people, Tom could tell Judy was becoming angry. Her body language and facial expressions clearly telegraphed impatience. Tom continued around the room to Will, who quietly said, "I'm concerned that we have so much work that we can't enter the data correctly even if we wanted to." Finally, Judy exploded by saying, "That's not true! That's simply not true!" Will immediately slumped down in this chair and stared at the floor.

Tom went on to the next person, who said, "Pass." And the next person, who said, "I'll pass." And the next said the same. And the next, too. Tom looked back at Judy and said nothing. She looked bewildered.

The Problem

Tom knew that any trust in the room had evaporated with Judy's outburst.

Members of the group were no longer willing to share their feeling and thoughts about the issue. Judy knew that she had spoken out of turn and she had criticized Will's feelings. The "safe zone" offered by the facilitation process was gone. Any openness within the meeting was gone, also.

What Happened?

Tom allowed Judy to criticize Will's concern. *By doing so, Tom actions said to group "Hey - it's OK for the boss to criticize you in this meeting... so you better be careful what you say!"*

Tom should have *immediately* stopped Judy by saying, "Judy, our process does not allow any criticism of concerns." Then Tom should have reinforced his words by pointing to the wall where a flipchart was taped, saying "Rule #6 - No criticism of concerns or possibilities".

The Lesson

Not only did Will stop talking but the entire group also stopping sharing their feelings. *And Tom lost some of his credibility as a neutral facilitator.*

Experience has shown that almost always *people only want an opportunity to express what's on their minds.* It's as simple as that. Too often, supervisors and managers are afraid that groups will use facilitated sessions to promote actions that are contrary to the welfare of the business. Again, experience has shown that they don't. People only want a chance to say what's on their minds. And collecting concerns is a step that provides each person with a safe, non-judgmental environment to express their inner feelings.

So, why is expressing these inner feelings so important to the process? First, it gives people like Will, who are reticent but *may* have a helpful perspective on the issue, an opportunity to share a unique point of view. Second, it provides a stage, or even a "soapbox", for team members to once-and-for-all tell the group (and the supervisor!) how they really feel... and then be finished. Third, it provides a checklist to verify that the group's action will satisfy the concerns of the group.

When you facilitate a group, do the following items during the *concerns* step:

1. Tell the group, "Concerns are your personal thoughts, feelings, or reflections. They are *your* concerns... *not someone else's* concerns."

2. Reinforce the rule of "no criticism."

3. Suggest that each person express her or his concern starting with "I feel..." or "I think..." or "I'm concerned about...".

4. If anyone says "I disagree..." or "I don't think so..." or any other form of criticism - STOP THEM IMMEDIATELY! Any criticism at this point of the process is a plague that causes silence and it spreads like wildfire!

5. Be careful that <u>you</u> as facilitator don't criticize! After a person offers a concern don't respond by saying, "That's good" or "Good thought" or "Great!".

   Remember: criticism can be positive as well as a negative!

CONCERNS

OUR CONCERNS ABOUT THE ISSUE:

- I worry about....
- I feel that....
- I think....
- I'm concerned about...

Solutions & Concerns

It doesn't matter Can concerns be solutions? Consider the following comments made by participants during the concerns phase of the session:

• "I think we should buy a newer computer."

• "I'm concerned about the money we spend on copier maintenance and we should buy a new copier."

The first is clearly a solution. The second is a mix of concern and solution. Should the facilitator say "Stop!" and correct these participants by saying, "I only want concerns, not solutions!!" The answer is no. Write whatever the participant says. Do not say "that's a solution" or "that's an action item." There must be no judgement by anyone in the room, especially the facilitator. Simply write the comment on the flipchart sheet and move onto the next person.

The kindness trap The facilitator is considered to be the role model for the group and always tries to act in a civil, courteous manner. Such behavior includes the appropriate "thank you" and "please." And trying to be even more kind, facilitators frequently respond with "That's a good idea" or "Excellent!" or "Very good" to comments made by participants. That's a mistake! Don't do it! Saying these nice things quickly removes the facilitator from the neutral role — regardless of any good intentions. This lesson is a word to the wise facilitator.

Review

Concerns

• Concerns are an essential step in opening up the group and allowing the participants to examine their feelings about the issue.

• Protect each participant from criticism while sharing his or her concerns. Failure to do so will most likely cause the participant to withhold his or her thoughts — and possibly begin a withdrawal from the process.

• Concerns should be written on a flipchart. No interpretation or analysis is permitted, only the facilitator's question, "Did I capture your concern correctly?"

• Use the list of concerns as a check in the final step. In the end of the process, compare the action items (or recommendations) with the concerns to see if everyone's concerns have been addressed.

And remember...

• Sometimes, all that someone wants is the chance to express an opinion. The concerns step provides that opportunity. Frequently in life and work, people never have the forum to tell how they feel about an issue. Collecting concerns is an invaluable step in providing that forum. It is remarkable how people, once allowed to speak their mind without criticism by anyone in the room, become ardent supporters of finding a shared solution to a problem.

"An idea is the brain's most perishable commodity."
— **John Boswell**

"Nothing is so exhausting as indecision, and nothing as futile."
— **Bertrand Russell**, *The Conquest of Happiness*, 1930

6 POSSIBLE SOLUTIONS?

People working in groups can create an amazing number of possible solutions. Far more, I believe, than an individual can alone.

Possible solutions, or possibilities, are the foundation for new and creative approaches to addressing the issue. Open, free-wheeling brainstorming is an easy and fun way for groups to generate numerous innovative answers.

As the third step in the facilitation process, developing possibilities is the most energizing. The facilitator should shepherd the process with lots of ENERGY! This is an opportunity for the facilitator to be a role model... get excited, be energetic, and throw out a few examples to "seed" the group's thoughts. Increase your tempo, be upbeat, and challenge individuals to suggest the craziest ideas on how to solve the problem!

These possibilities will be the basis for your action items in Step Five. So encourage the group to generate as many ideas as possible. Remember... anything goes! And no judging of ideas! And no criticism of ideas!

Let's go!

1 Issue?

2 Concerns	3 Possibilities
5 Action	4 Criteria

6 Check?

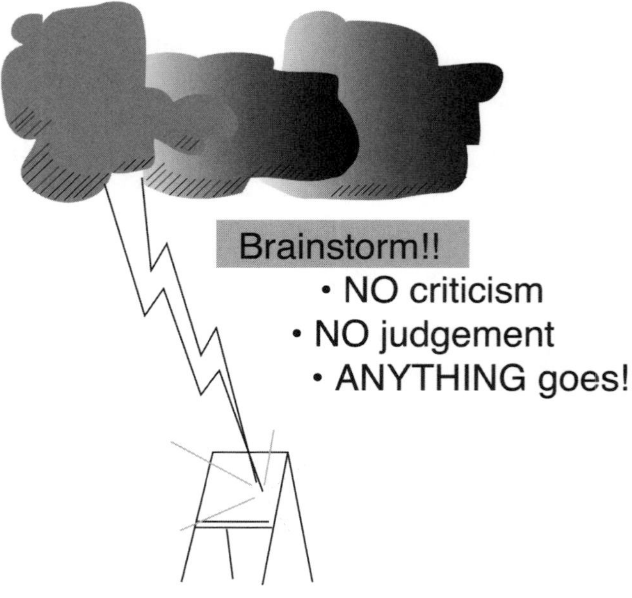
Brainstorm!!
• NO criticism
• NO judgement
• ANYTHING goes!

Brainstorming is one way to get a group's synergy into full production creating new and previously unconsidered solutions.

Start this step by explaining the rules:

- One person speaks at a time
- No criticism of other people's ideas
- OK to ask for clarification of an idea
- Building upon ideas is encouraged

Use a flipchart to record the possibilities.

Watch out Don't get caught in the trap of analyzing any possibility "as to whether or not it pertains to the issue." That is judging. Just write down the individual's suggestion and keep moving! In Step Four, the group's criteria will sort out any possibilities not addressing the issue... for now, you want to keep up the momentum and keep people popping out ideas!

Go! go! go! Keep the pace snappy! Throw out some ideas of your own as an example to help the group along.

TIP **Have someone be the "scribe" and write the possibilities on the flipchart. This will free you to keeping the group's energy up and ideas flowing!**

1 Issue?

2 Concerns	3 Possibilities
5 Action	Criteria 4

6 Check?

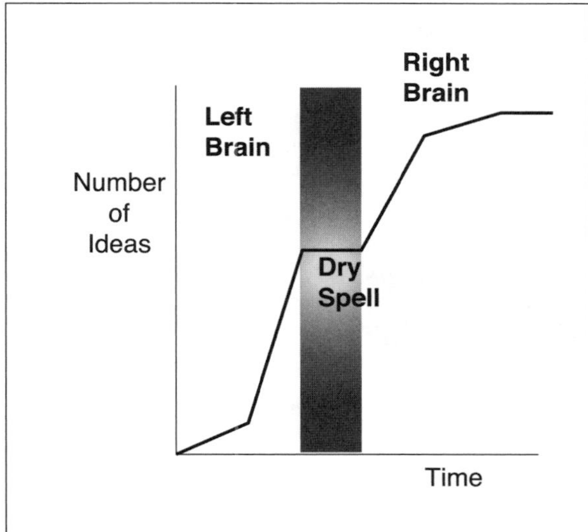

How Groups
Brainstorm Ideas Over Time

Ideas from a group come in three phases.

Logical ideas During the first phase, individuals draw solutions from their logic. This involves looking at the issue or problem and developing an answer from an analytical perspective. We commonly call this a "left brain" approach — that is, solutions are a result of a sequential analysis of the problem. This is a very natural way for most people to solve problems.

During this first phase, you as facilitator will be given many "common sense" solutions. Typically there will be nothing too surprising or too radical presented by the group.

Second phase Soon these possibilities using logical solutions will trickle to an end. And then there will be silence in the room. Don't be fooled into stopping this process step by saying, "Well, I guess that's all the possibilities!"

Keep going! When someone says, "That's all!" — don't stop! Instead, allow for the silence to continue. Wait several minutes if necessary. It may be uncomfortable, but there is something going on within the heads of each individual in the room.

During this second phase, everyone in the group has exhausted his or her inventory of logical, left-brained ideas. So, now the logical (left) part of the brain is soliciting input from the emotional and creative (right) side. Hence, silence in the room!

Silence pays off After agonizing minutes of silence, the participants will spurt with very creative possibilities! In this third phase, the group is pouring forth wacky, crazy ideas by using the right-side of their brains. By waiting through the group's silence, you now have tapped the creative side of the group. People will offer some strange possibilities... and then others in the room will build on them! Great!! Keep the momentum going at a quick pace until you drain every idea from the team.

TIP **Explain to the group how the left and right sides of the brain contribute ideas during this process. Warn the group that there will be a period of silence and that it is a very natural occurrence.**

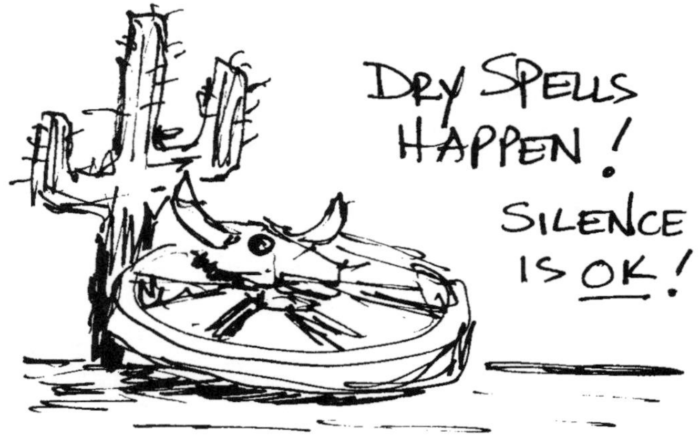

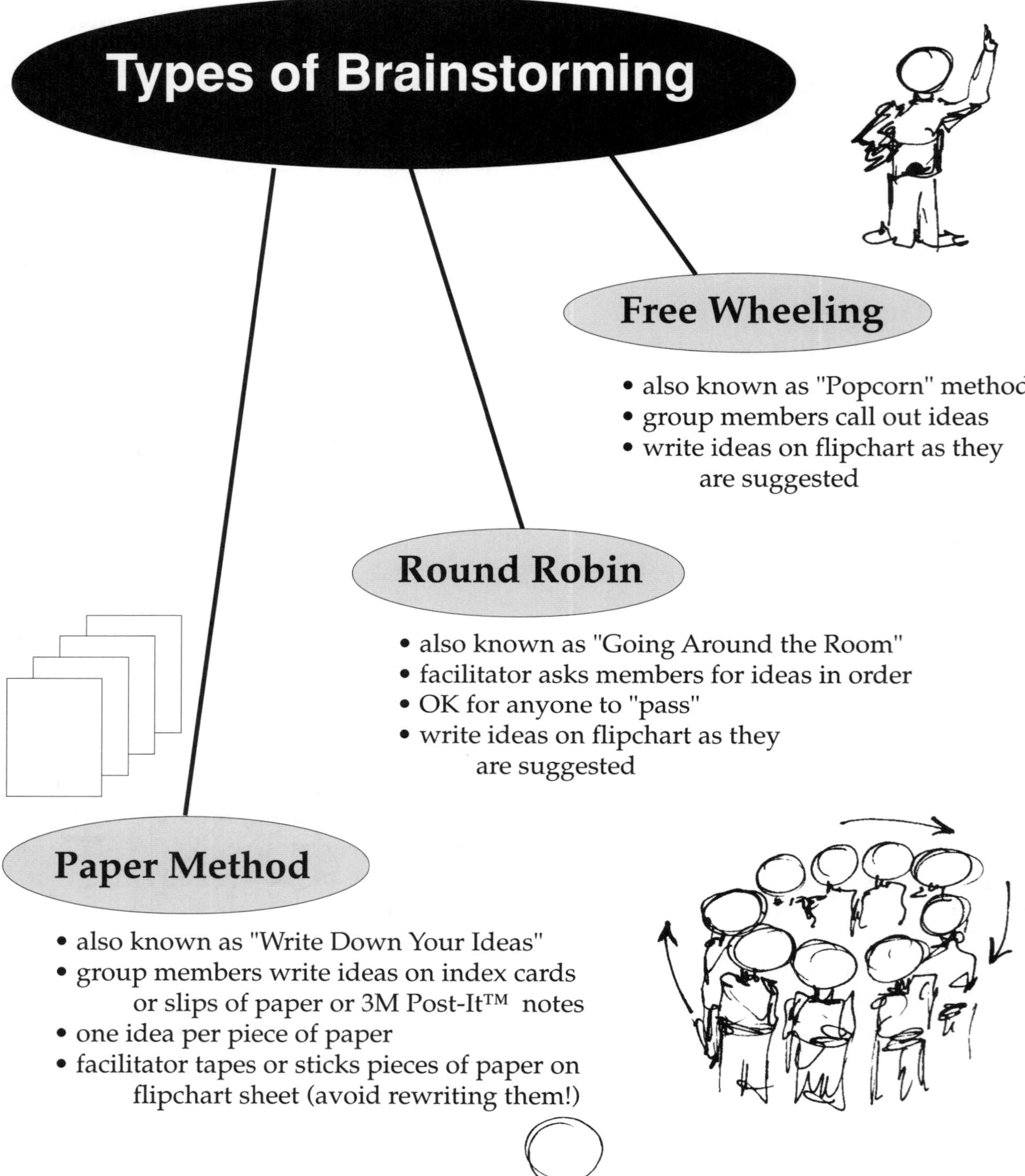
Types of Brainstorming
Free Wheeling
• also known as "Popcorn" method
• group members call out ideas
• write ideas on flipchart as they are suggested
Round Robin
• also known as "Going Around the Room"
• facilitator asks members for ideas in order
• OK for anyone to "pass"
• write ideas on flipchart as they are suggested
Paper Method
• also known as "Write Down Your Ideas"
• group members write ideas on index cards or slips of paper or 3M Post-It™ notes
• one idea per piece of paper
• facilitator tapes or sticks pieces of paper on flipchart sheet (avoid rewriting them!)

Rules for Brainstorming!!

Build on the ideas of others!

Make ideas clear and talk in "headlines"

Encourage everyone to participate!

Don't judge, criticize, or evaluate ideas!

Have fun! Get those creative juices flowing!

Write down every idea... no matter how crazy!

Generate as many ideas as possible... strive for a large QUANTITY of possibilities!

Case Study: What are the possibilities?

Background

Owen was brilliant. But he never learned how to shut up.

Owen was the current leader of the plant's Control Support Team. Being the chief CST member was a big responsibility because plant profitability was a direct result of the control computer's operation. He worked with nine other CST members, all providing 24 hour technical support for plant operators.

Several months ago, a management consultant met with the CST to conduct upwards-feedback sessions. One of the outputs of these sessions was the recommendation to create better relations between the CST and internal customers. Acting on this recommendation, Owen called Tom to facilitate a meeting of the team to decide on how to improve customer relations.

At one o'clock Tom began the meeting. Eight CST members were in attendance including Owen. Tom quickly moved through the preliminary elements of issue, stakeholders, communications, and concerns. Within an hour of the meeting's start, Tom had began brainstorming possibilities.

After fifteen minutes of round-robin brainstorming, the group fell quiet. Tom felt the uneasiness in the room but purposely said nothing.

"Come on, Tom," Owen said, finally cracking the silence. "Let's hurry up and get through this!" His impatience was undisguised as he continued, "We've all done this before, Tom. What's the delay?"

Tom was about to respond but Owen spoke first.

"We've got a turnover meeting in thirty minutes. The next shift will be coming on and we've got to be there during the turnover," Owen blurted out. "Can't we end this brainstorming now?"

Everyone stared at Owen. No one said a word.

The Problem

Tom now realized that Owen had a time constraint previously unknown to him. It governed Owen's perception of the meeting's timing and caused him to lash out at the facilitator when things were going too slowly. Sadly, Tom was never told about it and was caught off-guard.

Any creative spirit in the room was now gone. Owen's impatient outburst not only violated several meeting rules but also squelched the group's upbeat feelings, or eustress, that is essential for brainstorming.

What Happened?

Reflecting on the day later that evening, Tom determined that two key elements caused the breakdown in the facilitation. First, Owen's anxiety over attending the turnover meeting overpowered his need to appear supportive of the facilitation process. Second, Owen failed to share with Tom the need to finish the session before the two-thirty Operations turnover meeting.

The Lesson

After additional reflection that evening, Tom made a mental note to himself of things he would do in the future:

1. During the pre-meeting discussion with the leader, he would ask the leader if there are any time limits on the sessions. *And not ask it just once but several times...* to be certain the leader hasn't forgotten anything.

2. If ever interrupted by someone during a meeting (like Owen's outburst) over the facilitation process, *he would announce a short time-out*. Not only would this recess provide an opportunity to discuss any difficulties but the intermission would help "cool off" the interrupter.

3. If a solution couldn't be reached during the time-out then the facilitation process should be adjourned and another meeting time set to continue the process. Why? *If the disruption to the group's brainstorming was significant enough, then it would be very difficult to restore the eustress in the room.* The best plan would be let any hostilities subside and start the brainstorming again later.

The Silence Hurdle to Creativity

Almost physically painful It is one of the most uncomfortable phases in facilitation. Groups hate silence. Participants squirm in their seats. Eyes stare at the floor, the ceiling, the table — anywhere but at the facilitator. They are mortified to have such a vacuum in their world so typically filled with chatter.

It is necessary Some participants have begged — pleaded — to continue with the process and end the brainstorming. But don't do it. Let the silence continue. Allow for several minutes of quiet (it will seems like *years* instead of minutes) and then ask, "Any more ideas?" And then the ideas will come. At first a trickle of the absurd and outrageous ones. Then the pace will increase and participants will fling out ideas of surprising imagination. They will build upon the ideas of others to construct possible solutions previously unheard of!

Keep going After a flipchart page or two of ideas, the flow will decrease and trickle to a stop. Once again, give the group a minute of silence. Look at each participant. Standing in front of the room, be silent. After 60 more agonizing seconds, ask, "Any more?" If not, then stop.

Want more information about participation? See Chapter 17, "Getting Participation."

Review

Possible Solutions

• Brainstorming possibilities has one firm rule that the facilitator must enforce: NO CRITICISM of ideas!

• Brainstorming always has a "dry spell"

• The facilitator is smart to "uncomfortable silence" during brainstorming to help the group generate more ideas

• Have a scribe help you record ideas — it helps with the flow of brainstorming

And remember...

• Prime the pump by giving examples of wacky ideas. Show participants that it's OK to suggest out-of-this-world ideas during the brainstorming portion of the process.

• Sometimes it is helpful to explain to the group that switching from the left (logical) side of the brain to the right (creative) side will happen during brainstorming and not to be discouraged when the first flow of ideas stops.

"It's what you learn after you know it all that counts."
— **John Wooden**

> "Men and melons are hard to know."
> — **Benjamin Franklin,** *Poor Richard's Almanac*

7 CRITERIA?

This is the rationale This is an important step. The group's criteria list "sets the stage" for determining action steps necessary to address the issue. They also help the group explain to outsiders and stakeholders the rationale of why (or why not) the group choose specific actions.

These criteria set the group's boundaries of acceptable action. Any brainstormed possibility that fails to satisfy the criteria cannot become an action item.

Realistic criteria It is important that the group be flexible and be willing to revisit its criteria list. As the group's discussion proceeds, individuals will discover that either some criterion is not realistic or that additional ones are needed.

The facilitator should challenge the group to closely examine the validity of any criterion adopted. This step requires time and it is frequently skimmed-over because the group is impatient to get to the action items. The facilitator must insist that the group take the time to complete this important step.

1 Issue?

2 Concerns	3 Possibilities
5 Action	4 Criteria

6 Check?

TIP **Start with the Basic Criteria and ask the group if they would like to add or delete criterion. If the group is at a loss for other criteria, suggest some criterion from the advanced list.**

Criteria act as the "strainer" for the group's possibilities. Those possibilities that meet the criteria will "pass through" and become action items.

It is during this exercise that the group may realize that their criteria list is incorrect or incomplete. You as the facilitator should accommodate any changes in the criteria list that the group desires.

Basic Criteria

Whatever the group decides to do, that action must:

- Be legal and moral
- Be achievable
- Be understandable to all others
- Meet the needs of the issue
- Recognize limited resources available

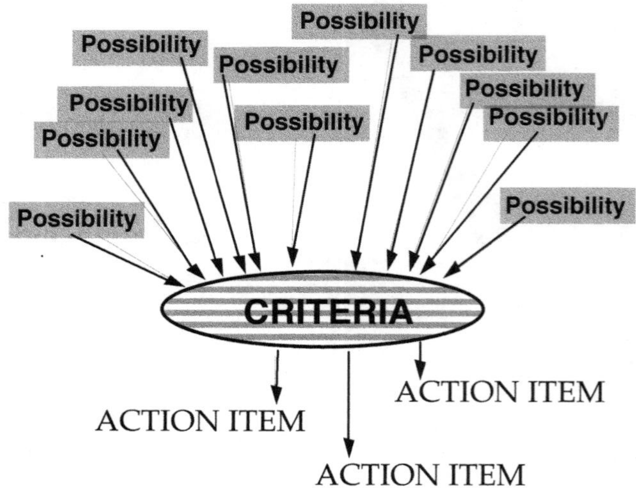

1 Issue?

2 Concerns	3 Possibilities
5 Action	Criteria 4

6 Check?

Advanced Criteria

Whatever the group decides to do, that action must:

• Support and be consistent with our organization's vision & mission

• Consider the adverse impact on ourselves and on others

• Be cost effective

• Have a clear owner

• Have results which are measurable

• Meet any contractual obligations

• Allow for input from concerned individuals and organizations

• Address long-term implications as well as short-term needs

• Have a clear focus

• Consider a life cycle - when does it end?

• Recognize company needs and strategies

• Be manageable

• Have customer approval and buy-in

• Be K.I.S.S. - as simple as possible

• Add value

• Be consistent and fair to all persons involved

• Incorporate some feedback process

• Cause resolution of the problem in a timely manner

Our Criteria
Legal & Moral
Cost Effective
Achievable
Measurable
Fun
Meets the needs

Creating the Group's Criteria List

Step One

•Use the **Basic Criteria** and **Advanced Criteria** lists as resources for suggesting possible criterion to the group.

Step Two

•List all possible criterion suggested by the group.

Step Three

•Use consensus-building tools to obtain the group's final Criteria List.

Possible Criterion - p. 1

- makes money
- achievable
- understandable to all?
- meets customers' needs?
- allows us to have fun?
- no impact on budget
- supports union contract

Possible Criterion - p. 2

- helps get me promoted
- is legal & moral
- has clear owner
- has customer buy-in
- supports Co. mission
- supports our vision
- adds value
- manageable
- incorporates feedback

Possible Criterion - p. 3

- has an end to it
- passes "bulletin-board test"
- is simple
- can be measured
- fair to everyone
- cost effective
- does not violate any Company policies

Our CRITERIA

Whatever we do, it will...

- be legal & moral
- satisfy the customers' needs
- be cost-effective
- meet Company policies

Case Study: What are our criteria?

Background
Tom stood at the flipchart easel with his back to the group. Turning his head to face them, he asked, "OK, let's list some criteria for deciding our action. Anyone want to start?"

Silence. He turned and faced them. He repeated, "Anyone? Any criteria or rules to judge our possibilities?"

Enough of the room looked lost that Tom stopped. He put the marker pen down and walked to the center of the room.

"I sense that no one has the energy to keeping going," he said. "Should we stop for today? We can meet tomorrow at one o'clock."

No one spoke.

Curious, Tom looked at Sandy and asked, "Sandy, what would you like to do now?"

For the first time since Tom's monologue began she looked at Tom and replied, "I'm lost. I don't know what we should be doing now... I mean, how are we going to sort through eight flipcharts of possibilities?"

"Yeah. It's just too overwhelming, Tom," Burt called out from the back of the room, "we've got all these possibilities and we're no closer to solving our problem than when we started!"

Tom nodded his head. "I understand," he said. "Let's take a fifteen minute break... be back at two forty-five."

The Problem
Many, if not all, of the team members were *frustrated* with their progress towards solving the problem outlined in their issue statement. They had lost sight of the process steps following the brainstorming of the possibilities step.

What Happened?

Tom was embarrassed with himself because he had assumed the group understood the importance of the *criteria step*. They did not.

Pulling open his facilitation binder, he found a list of possible criteria for the group. He wrote several of them on a blank flipchart sheet:

- Measurable
- Legal & moral
- Not cause us to exceed our expense budget
- Satisfies Company policies
-
-
-

These would serve as "seeds" for the group to create their own list of criteria. The three bullets with blanks afterwards would be spaces he'd write in the group's own criteria.

At two forty-five, Tom restarted the meeting by announcing, "Here's a sample list of criteria for us to consider." He pointed to the flipchart he'd prepared during the break. "Please read them."

Tom continued, "OK, now. Remember that the criteria you select will be the rules, or test, for each of the possibilities. If any possibility doesn't meet the criteria then it can't become part of the group's action plan."

"Questions?" he asked. "Great. Sandy, finish this sentence for me: *'Whatever we do, it will...'* "

Sandy winced. After a few moments she replied, "...meet the operating guidelines of the plant." She immediately repeated, "Whatever we do will meet the operating guidelines of the plant."

"Good!" Tom said, "Now, Burt, you finish the same sentence for us: *'Whatever we do, it will...'* "

The Lesson

Take the time to explain the concept of criteria to the group. Too often, facilitators assume that everyone understands this process step. Although all human beings use criteria constantly during their waking hours to decide personal actions, we forget how to purposely apply them in formal facilitations.

Do this during the criteria step:

1. Explain how the group's *criteria is important* to sorting out its possibilities.

2. Show some *example criteria* from a standard list.

3. Prime the group for their suggestions by *phrasing your question* as, "Whatever we do, it will..."

4. After listing everyone's suggestions for criteria, start at the top of the list and *obtain their consensus* for each one. If the group can't support a criteria, then discard it.

5. Don't be surprised if, as the action items are being built in the following step, *the group wishes to revise its list of criteria* and go back to reconsider some previously discarded possibilities. *This desire is natural* and reassessing criteria, at any time, is an acceptable process step.

Our CRITERIA

Whatever we do, it will...
- be legal & moral
- satisfy the customers' needs
- be cost-effective
- meet Company policies

Specific Criteria

Not groundrules Remember that criteria are not groundrules for the participants' conduct. They are boundaries for identifying acceptable actions, recommendations, or alternatives. Whereas groundrules are somewhat general (*"One person talks at a time"*), criteria must be as specific as possible.

Specific criteria speed the process Force the group to pinpoint their criteria. Doing so will greatly help when you use them to eliminate unqualified possibilities. Vague criteria result in participants interpreting them differently and cause time-wasting discussions. Consider the examples below.

General	Specific
Whatever we do, it will be...	*Whatever we do, it will be...*
1. Cost effective	1. Cost less than $100,000 in 2003
2. Done in a timely manner	2. Finished by November 1, 2005
3. Meet the needs of our customer	3. Provide 90% customer satisfaction in 2003
4. Completed in a professional manner	4. Prepared by a licensed Civil Engineer
5. Easy to repair	5. Require no more than 5 man-days maintenance each year.
6. Attractive to the public	6. Meet county zoning laws and approved by the county planning commission
7. Easy to implement	7. Designed and built within three months
8. Profitable	8. Provide a 22% return on capital employed (after taxes)

Review

Criteria

• Criteria are the "filter" that possibilities must successfully pass through before becoming action items or recommendations.

• Criteria are excellent reasons for answering the question, "How'd you come up with that action (or recommendation)?

• The best criteria are specific ones — always force the group to use numbers, dates, or quantifiable descriptions in its criteria.

And remember...

• Do NOT skip the criteria step! Seed the group with the standard criterion that every group should (I hope) have: *legal & moral.*

• To help the group understand the role of criteria in the facilitation process, say aloud this phrase before each criteria, "Whatever we do, it will be (the criteria)." For example, say "Whatever we do, it will be legal and moral." Or, "Whatever we do, it will not cost more than $10 million during the calendar year." This preamble greatly helps participants understand the role of criteria in the process.

"All of us are self-centered, suckers for a bit of praise."
— **Tom Peters & Robert H. Waterman, Jr.**

"To get something done a committee should consist of no more than three men, two of whom are absent."
— **Robert Copeland**

8 ACTION?

Why action? Some form of action is the desired output of every group. This output could be a list of recommendations, a matrix of action items or a summary of alternatives.

Dangerous jumping In our society, we have a bias towards action. Unfortunately, most groups jump from *concerns* (Step Two) directly to *action* (Step Five) without the benefits of (1) identifying the issue, (2) brainstorming possibilities for solutions, or (3) agreeing on the criteria for selecting the action items. Such haste typically results in action that fails to solve the problem and forces the group to spend more time later trying to develop some other plan of attack to rectify the issue.

This process avoids that dilemma. After a group agrees on its criteria in Step Four, it is then possible to screen the list of possibilities for acceptable solutions. By applying the criteria to each possibility generated in Step Three, the group creates a list of potential action items.

1 Issue?

2 Concerns	3 Possibilities
5 Action	4 Criteria

6 Check?

Recommendations The same process would be used to create an output of recommendations or alternatives.

What to do...

1 • Hang the possibilities flipchart sheets on a wall in front of the group

2 • Start with the first possibility. Ask the group "Does this possibility satisfy our criteria?"

3 • If the group agrees that it satisfies the criteria then quickly move on to the next possibility and repeat the question.

4 • If the group does not agree that the possibility meets the criteria, then cross out the item and move on to the next one.

5 • After going through the entire list of possibilities, go back and group together any that are similar.

6 • After completing this grouping, select one group and build an action item.

7 • Continue building action items from the groups until finished. Remember that action items answer "what", "who", and "when".

8 • The next step is to check your action against the concerns raised in Step Two.

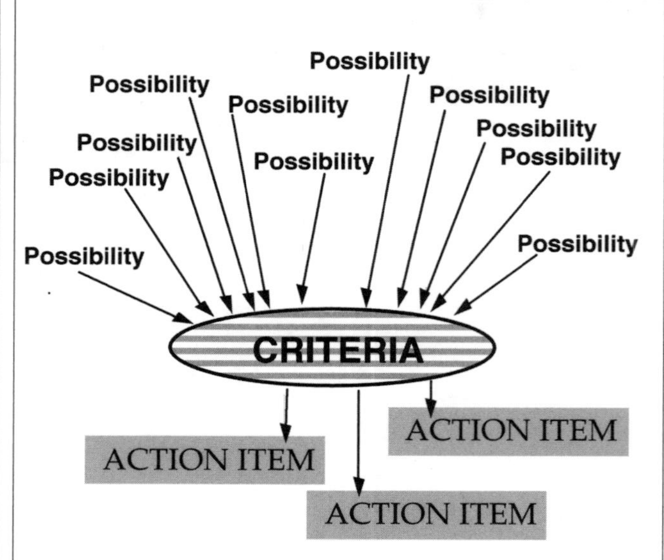

1 Issue?

2 Concerns	3 Possibilities
5 Action	4 Criteria

6 Check?

Case Study: What's our action plan?

Background

The group was returning from a fifteen minute break. Three of the team members were standing near the door talking.

"This is really stupid, Tom. We've spent three meetings on this issue and all we have to show for it are twelve pages of alternatives!" Hal complained.

"If you had listened at the start of all this, Hal, then you'd know that we won't do *each* of them," Brenda interrupted. "We'll only do the ones that meeting our criteria."

"It's no different than how you decided what to do in your own life, Hal," Barry quipped, "you have dozens of criteria that you use to sort out what's your next step."

"Yeah," Brenda added, "Like when you're trying to decide what to buy for lunch."

"What?" Hal winced as he replied, "How does my buying lunch have anything to do with solving our group's issue? You guys aren't making any sense!"

"Look here," Tom interjected, "Brenda and Barry have a important point. Let's use the group's criteria to eliminate the unacceptable possibilities."

"What do you mean?" Hal asked.

"Remember the list of criteria we just agreed on? You know, those statements saying 'Whatever we do, it will be legal and moral,' or '...it won't cause us to exceed our budget'," Tom said.

"I remember them clearly. But those are just our rules for whatever action we take, right?" Hal replied.

"Right! And to make sure of that, we use those criteria as tests for *each* of our possibilities. We'll go down the list of possibilities, all twelve pages of them, and test each one against the criteria. If a possibility doesn't satisfy all of our criteria we'll cross it off!" Tom instructed.

"OK. I see the value in doing that. But then what'll we do with the possibilities that made it through the criteria. Do we build action items out of them?" Hal asked.

"Bingo! Now you understand, Hal!" Brenda chimed it. "We'll take the possibilities that pass the criteria test and build action items out of them!"

"And remember what Tom told us... action items need to be specific, have an owner, and a time limit!" Barry added.

"Now I understand! Let's start building some action items!" Hal responded.

Tom called the team back together and announced that it was time to start building some action items.

"The vice president of manufacturing asked that we provide the plant management team with a list of specific tasks this team proposes to do to solve the issue. Are we ready to start converting all of our brainstormed possibilities into some action?" Tom asked.

"Let's do it!" Hal yelled with a smile.

The Problem

Hal, and maybe others in the group, felt overwhelmed because of the large quantity of possible solutions generated in the process. After several days of work, he and others felt no closer to solving the issue than at the start of the process. His frustration was obvious.

If not immediately addressed, Hal's frustration could have undermined the effectiveness of the team. Tom had seen this happen before when one or more team members cannot see the connection between the possibilities, criteria, and action item steps — and they become openly critical of the process.

What Happened?

Tom, as the facilitator, assumed that everyone understood the process steps necessary to reduce the possibilities into action items. At least one person, and possibly others, did not. *Tom should have spent more time repeating the steps of the process to assure that everyone understood.* Because experienced facilitators do the possibilities-criteria-action item sequence so frequently, they can mistakenly assume that everyone knows it equally well.

The Lesson

Do this: *three times* during the facilitation process remind the group of how action items are made : (1) *at the beginning* when first explaining the process, (2) once again *after brainstorming of possibilities*, and (3) finally, *after finishing the criteria step.*

When reminding the group, cover these three points:

1. Action Items are made of one or more possibilities *that satisfy the group's criteria.*

2. Action Items are the *final output* of the group. They are tasks involving activity by one or more people, usually group members.

3. Action Items must have three components: *what, who, & when.*

   What = specific task to be completed
   Who = person responsible for completion of the task
   When = latest date when the task must be completed

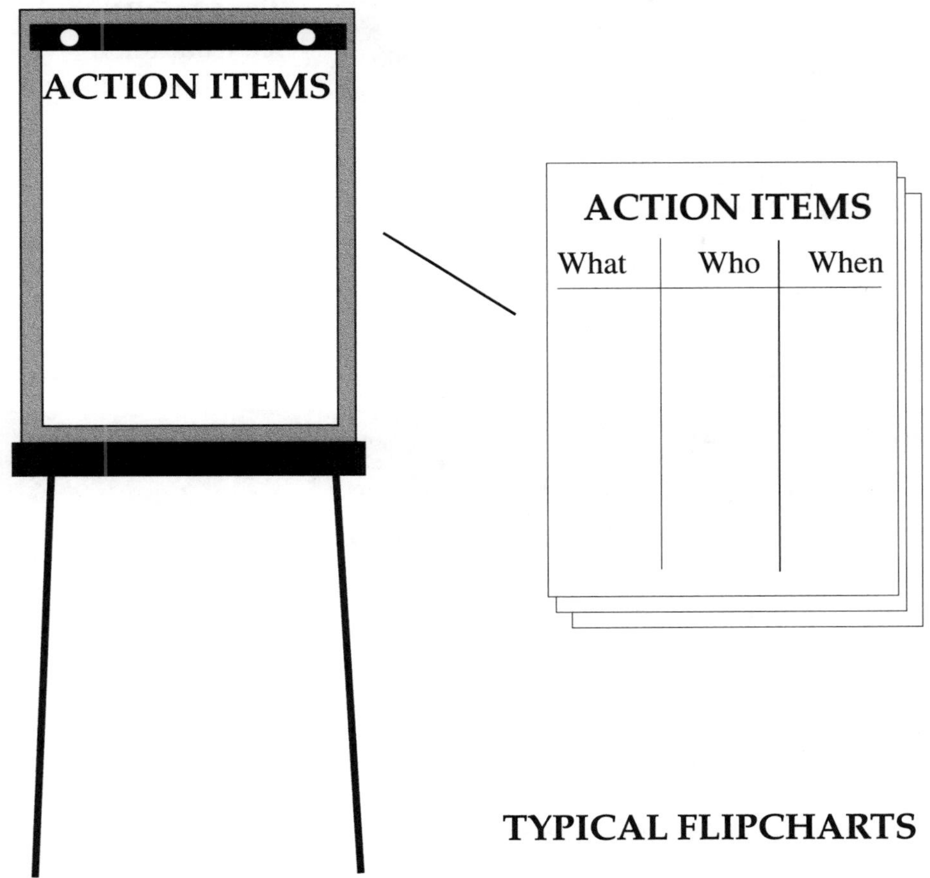

TYPICAL FLIPCHARTS

How do you get agreement on which possibilities satisfy the group's criteria?

Common understanding We mistakenly assume that everyone in the group fully understands each possibility. Do this: when you check a possibility, first ask the group, "Does anyone need more explanation about this possibility?" Wait five seconds to see if any clarification is needed. Then proceed to check the possibility against the group's criteria. Repeat this step for each possibility.

Consensus agreement Experience shows that consensus is the best method for group decision making (see box below). Having the leader simply decide whether a possibility becomes an action item (or recommendation, depending on the authority level of the group) is counterproductive — it defeats the benefits of group synergy and also demoralizes participants by robbing them of their power. By using a democratic process, the minority loses and support is therefore crippled. And trying to build an action list by unanimous decision is very, very time consuming — and nearly impossible to attain in a group.

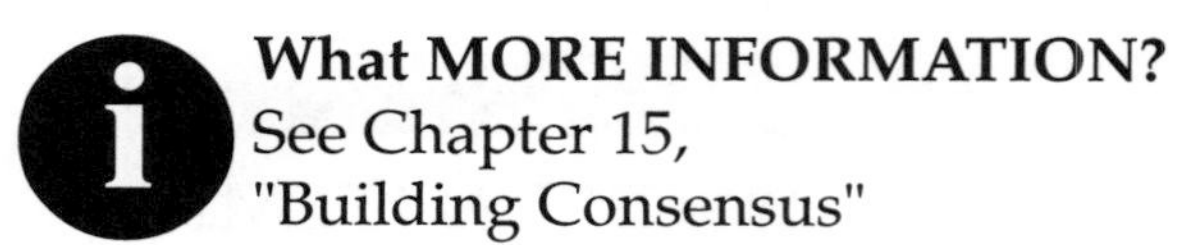
What MORE INFORMATION?
See Chapter 15, "Building Consensus"

Common Methods Used to Decide on Group Output

(action items, recommendations, or alternatives)

Autocratic (leader decides)

Democratic (group majority decides)

Consensus (each group member supports decision)

Unanimous (each group member agrees with decision)

Review

Action

• A group's output can be in the form of recommendations, alternatives, or action items.

• Always use criteria to judge which possibilities become the group's action items, recommendations, or list of alternatives.

• An action item list always has three parts:

- **What** has to be done
- **Who** will do it
- **When** will it be completed

And remember...

• Use group consensus to build the list of action items, recommendations, or alternatives.

"If you're yearning for the good old days, just turn off the air conditioning."
— **Griff Niblack**, *Indianapolis News*

> "I have a memory like an elephant. In fact, elephants often consult me."
>
> — **Noël Coward**

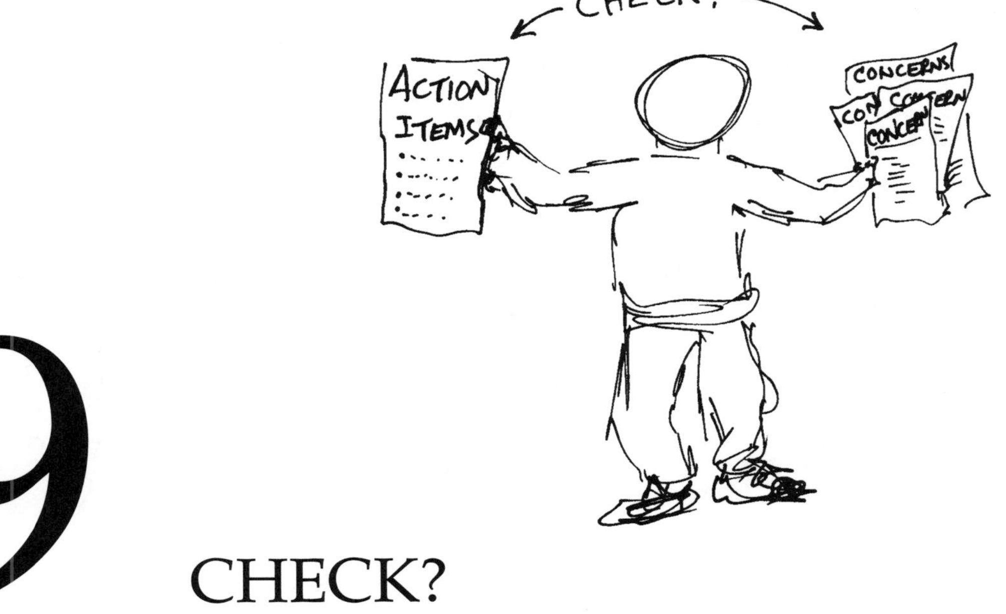

9 CHECK?

What's involved in this step? You and the group have spent many hours up this point working through this six step problem-solving process. How does the group know that its list of recommendations or actions address its concerns? Has the group achieved the leader's desired outcome(s)? What is the next step? How will the group communicate its results to outsiders?

The Check Step In this final step, you as facilitator will lead the group in doing four tasks: (1) checking actions against concerns, (2) checking if the leader's desired outcome(s) have been satisfied, (3) checking the next step for the group, and (4) checking the communications plan.

❶ Issue?

❷ Concerns	❸ Possibilities
❺ Action	❹ Criteria

❻ Check?

CHECK: Actions & Concerns

Why do it?

- It assures that action items address group concerns
- It provides closure on the process

How is it done?

- **Display** the group's original list of **concerns**.
- **Display** the group's list of **action items**.
- Start at Concern #1 and **ask the group**, "Do any of our action items address this concern?"
- If the answer is yes, **continue** to Concern #2
- If the answer is no, then ask the group, "Should we **modify** one of our action items or make a **new** action item to address this concern?" *Then do what the group decides. If an action item is modified or a new one created, make sure that it satisfies all criteria.*
- Continue through all concerns on the list in the same manner

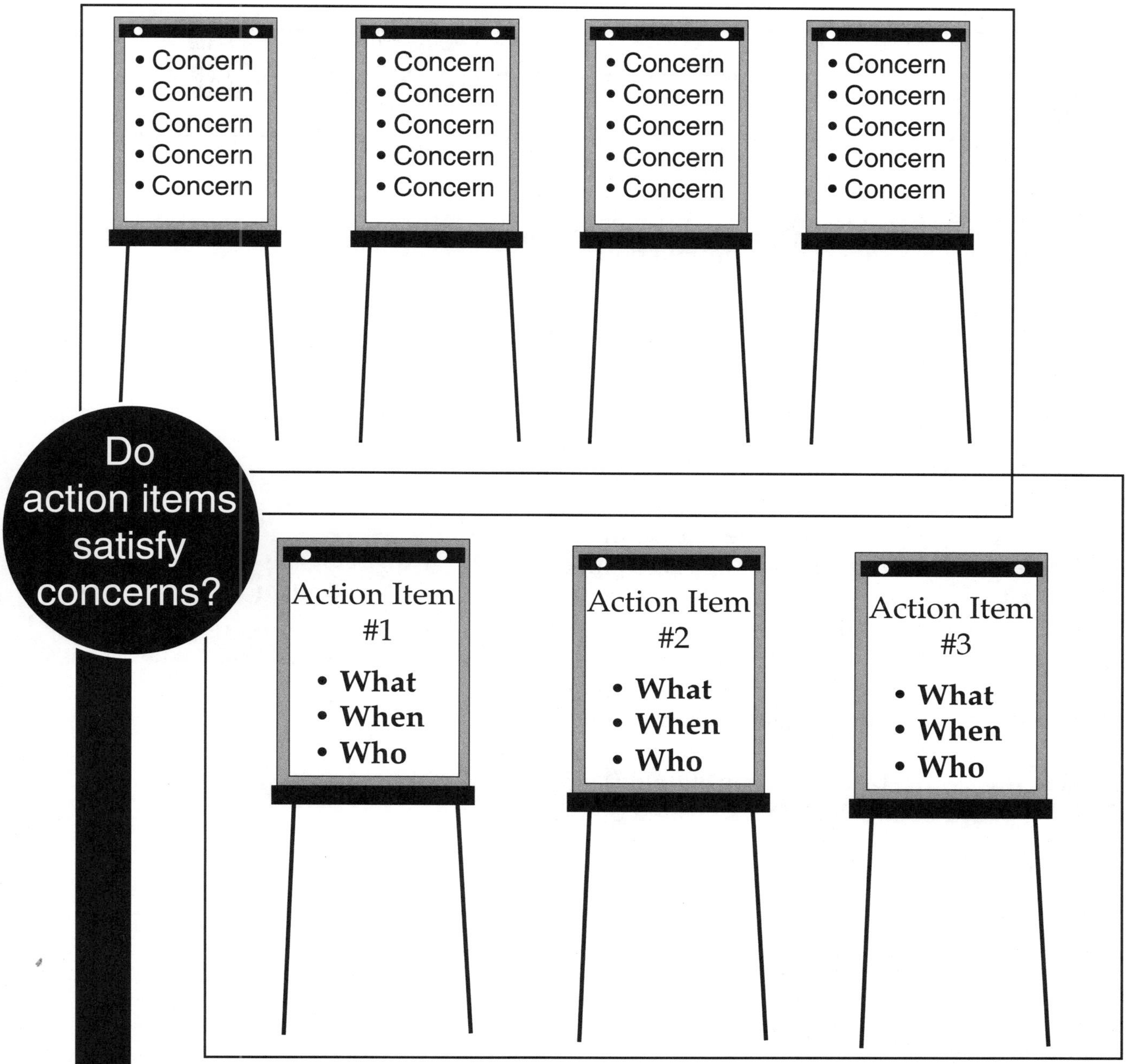

• Concern
• Concern
• Concern
• Concern
• Concern

• Concern
• Concern
• Concern
• Concern
• Concern

• Concern
• Concern
• Concern
• Concern
• Concern

• Concern
• Concern
• Concern
• Concern
• Concern

Do action items satisfy concerns?

Action Item #1
• **What**
• **When**
• **Who**

Action Item #2
• **What**
• **When**
• **Who**

Action Item #3
• **What**
• **When**
• **Who**

Why do a check? It is very important to always check the final action list against the initial concerns list. Such a check assures that each action item addresses the concerns of the group. If there are concerns left unaddressed by the action list, then it is appropriate for the facilitator to ask the group, "It looks like we didn't address this concern. Is there some action that we should add to the action list?" If so, then have the group work out the action item and add it to the action list (warning: make sure that this new action item satisfies the criteria adopted by group). In addition to catching an unaddressed concerns, a check also provides closure on the process.

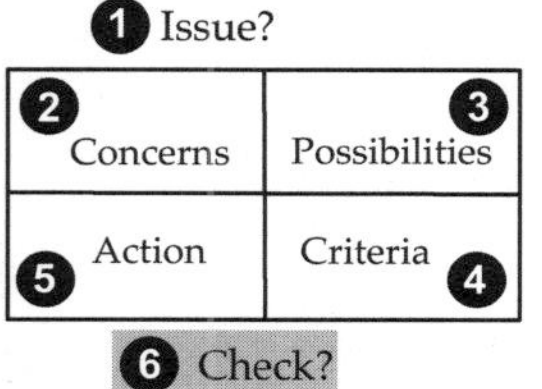

❷ CHECK: Desired Outcomes Met?

Second step After checking the action items against the group's concerns, your next task to do check to see if the group has satisfied the desired outcomes for the process. The outcomes were given to you by the leader before, or at, the first meeting.

Why is this important? Success in completing this problem-solving process is determined by meeting the leader's expectations. For example, the leader expected the group to create "a list of 10 to 20 action items." Your check uncovers a list of only three action items. Obviously, you have not met the leader's expectations and more work is required. As a second example, suppose the leader asked the group to provide a list of recommendation. Your check revealed only a single, specific action item was created. This would not satisfy the leader's request and more is work is likely required by the group.

HINT: The leader has the list of desired outcomes.

What to do As the facilitator, you should (1) make a flipchart paged listing the leaders desired outcomes, and (2) ask the group, "Do you feel that we have satisfied these expectations?"

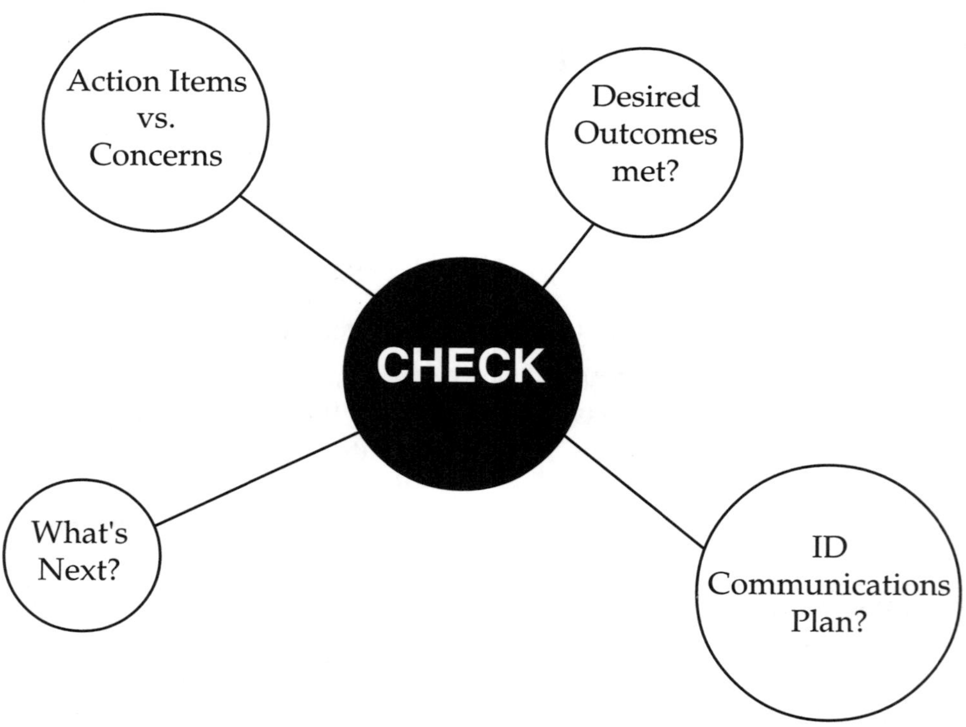

3 CHECK: What's The Next Step?

Ask the group, "What still needs to be done?"

Third step Is it time for cake and ice cream? Time for handshakes and hugs? Time for celebration and getting back to work? What is the group going to do now? One obvious next step is communicating the group's output (see *"4 - Check: Communications Plan?"* for more details). What else will the group do?

Next Step list As the facilitator, you can help the group decide on the next steps by asking the question, "What still needs to be done?" Then brainstorm a list of possibilities. Remember the list of desired outcomes that the leader gave to you before the first meeting? Now is the time to get it out and look at it. Use this list of desired outcomes as the "check" on the brainstormed list. Once checked, the final flipchart is called the Next Step list. Note that this list is similar to the action items list, containing three essential parts: the what, the who , and the when.

What to do First, incorporate the items on the Next Step list into the group's communication plan. Second, send copies of the Next Step list to the leader and all stakeholders.

OUR NEXT STEPS

WHAT	WHO	WHEN
1. Implement communications plan	Ken, Becky	End of Month
2. Hold celebration lunch	Dani	End of Week
3. Send "thank you" gift to leader	Suzie	End of Month
4. Take facilitator to dinner	Caroline	End of Month
5. Meet to evaluate progress of action items & communications plan	ALL	6 months from today

 CHECK: Communications Plan?

Final step OK. You've checked actions versus concerns, desired outcomes, and the group's next step. Now, how are you going to communicate what the group has accomplished?

Why is this important? You and the group have invested a great amount of time in this process. It is important to communicate (to employees, clients, management) what has been accomplished and how it was done. Why? First, the group's output is a valuable product and needs to be shared — and used. Second, the group's behaviors and output need to be visible as a desirable role model for other groups and employees. And third, the group's success needs to be celebrated.

What to do First, brainstorm a list of possibilities — possible communication tools, events, media, etc.

Second, agree on some criteria (how much money does the group have to spend? How much time is available? Who's our intended audience?

Third, use the criteria to create a communications action plan. Don't forget to use the "what," "who," and "when" structure.

OUR COMMUNICATIONS PLAN

1. Send emails to all employees.
   *Who:*________
   *When:*________
2. Hold informational meeting with every shift and crew.
   *Who:*________
   *When:*________
3. Hang posters in work areas. *Who:*________
   *When:*________

Communications Ideas

1. Company webpage
2. Special pamphlet mailed to employees' homes
3. Monthly company newsletter
4. Wall posters
5. Letter or memo
6. Information meetings
7. Videotaped presentation
8. Luncheon

Case Study: Shouldn't we do a check?

Background

Three weeks had passed since the team had issued its report. Nine distinct action items were reported to the plant, each with the objective of improving customer service. The team was happy with its work and very proud of the action plan it created for the plant.

However, Doug, an information systems supervisor, was not as satisfied as the team. At the weekly management team meeting, Doug raised his hand and asked, "Why didn't the team include some action on getting feedback from us on these nine items?"

"We talked a lot about getting feedback," Tom answered, "but I guess we neglected to include any specific process in our action items."

"Well that's pretty short sighted," Doug replied. "How can you expect to improve our customer service rating if we don't have any way to get feedback?"

Tom turned to Brenda, sitting next to him, and whispered, "Why didn't the group include something on feedback in their action plan?"

"Because we forgot. I didn't even think about it until now!" Brenda whispered back. "What should we do?"

"Good point, Doug," Tom said turning away from Brenda, "we should have included that concern in our action list. I guess we just made a mistake!"

"Tom, we talked about the importance of feedback during the concerns segment of our meetings," Brenda said quietly, "so why didn't anything on feedback show up in our action items?"

The Problem

The group's action items did not address one of their more important concerns: feedback to plant's management team. And it wasn't until three days later that this oversight was discovered.

What Happened?
Tom, as the group's facilitator, neglected to do a final "check" with the group to assure that all concerns had been met through the team's action items.

The Lesson
Most facilitators skip over this step because everyone is eager to wrap-up the meeting and "get back to work." Before adjourning, the facilitator should ask the group, *"Should we check our action items against the group's concerns? Let's be certain that the group's actions satisfy its concerns... would that be OK with everyone?"*

Do the following before disbanding the group:

1. *Review the original list of concerns.* If they are written on flipchart sheets, then tape them on the wall for everyone to see. If written on small sheets then make copies for each participant.

2. *Check to see if each concern is addressed by one of the action items.* A convenient method is to post the group's list of action items on the wall next to the list of concerns. Let the group have enough time to study both lists.

3. *Modify or add action items as necessary to cover any concerns not addressed.* It is the group's decision whether or not a concern is significant enough to either change an existing action item, create a new action item, or do nothing. Many times a group discovers a concern unaddressed by its action plan but may consider it not important enough to make any changes to the action item list.

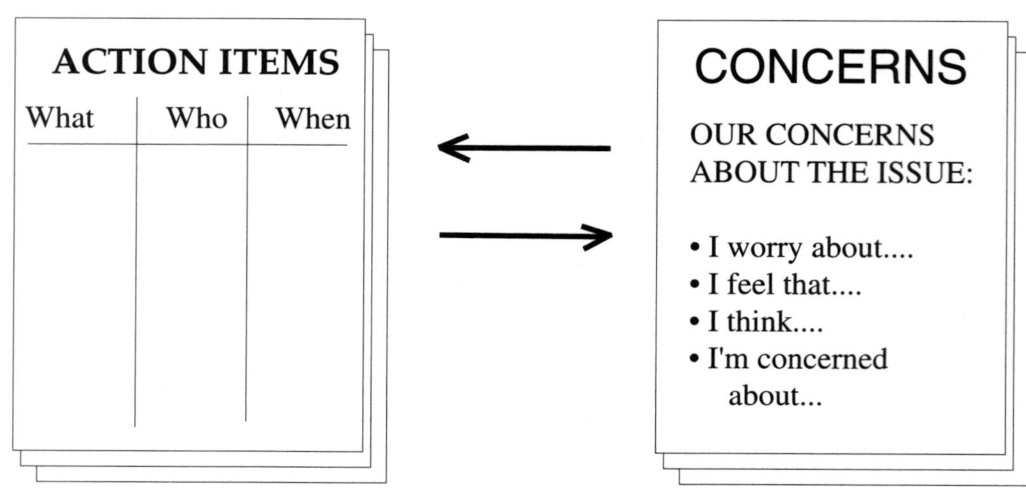

Review

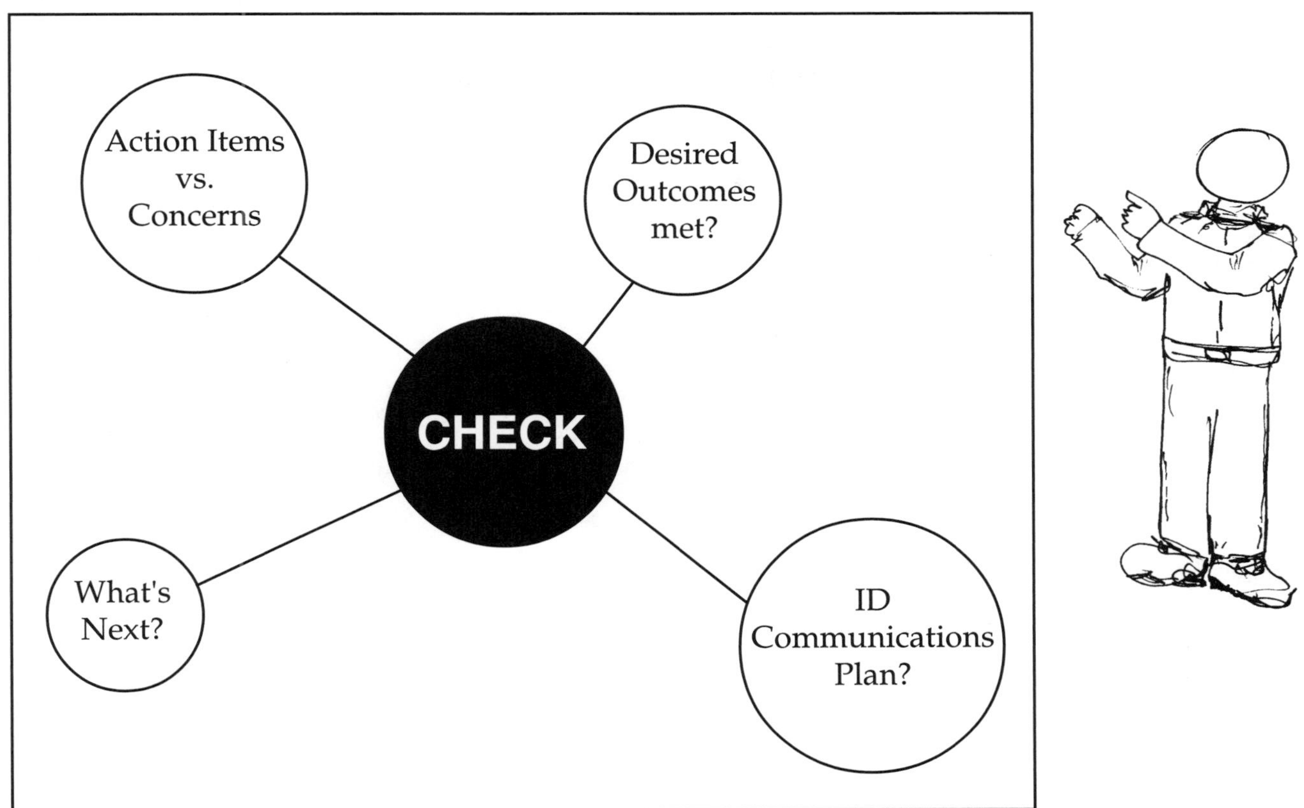

CHECK: Actions & Concerns

CHECK: Desired Outcomes Met?

CHECK: What's The Next Step?

CHECK: Communications Plan?

"We aim above the mark to hit the mark."
— **Ralph Waldo Emerson**

III

Doing It!

10. Getting **Started**
11. You And The **Leader**
12. Pre-Meeting **Logistics** & The Room
13. **Flipcharts** And Other Visual Tools
14. The **First** Meeting

"Every organization needs one core competence: innovation."
— **Peter Drucker**

> "There is no traffic jam on the extra mile."
> — **Dr. Aubrey Daniels**

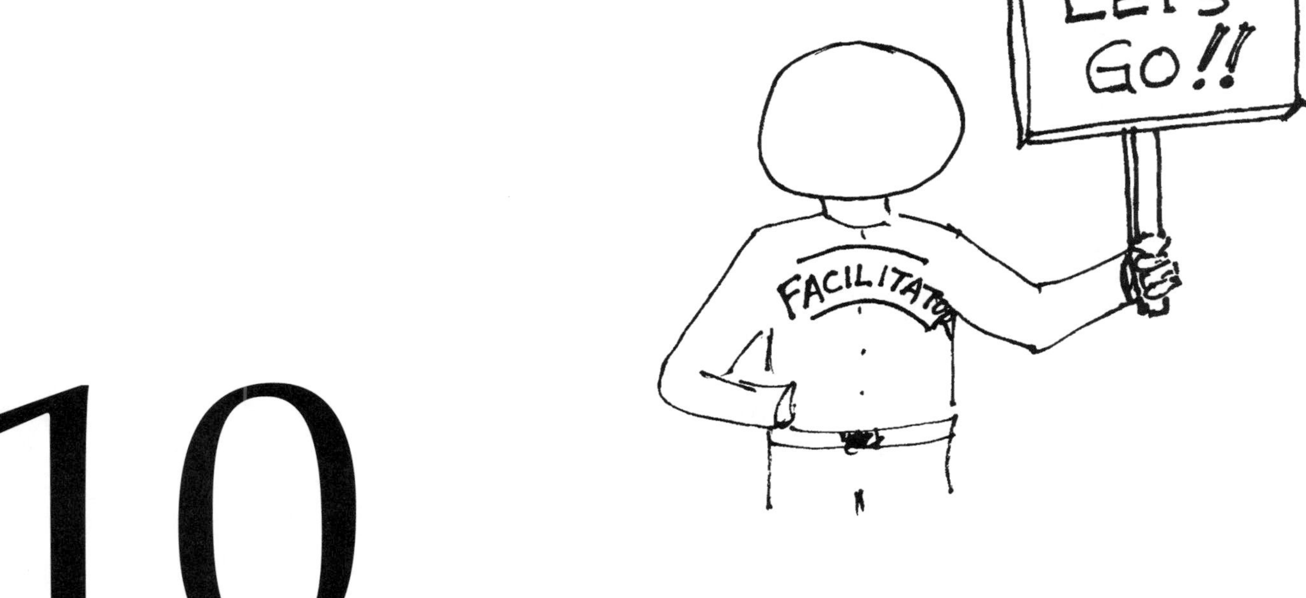

10 GETTING STARTED

What's involved? There is no substitute for experience. And good facilitators have plenty of it. To help you get started with your session, you need to prepare and investigate. Your preparation includes getting a great deal of background information about the issue, talking to people critical to the issue, and some logistical tasks involving the group's participants and the meeting room.

Your investigation focuses on the expectations of the leader and the identity of stakeholders. The leader is your first contact and your primary source of information. The timing, the group's authority level, the definition of success, and the pinpointed definition of the issue are examples of information you'll need to get started.

Is this preliminary stuff necessary? Only if you want to be successful. Experience has shown that facilitators who do not do the preliminary work noted in this chapter are doomed to muddle around in the process — a waste of everyone's time. If you think that you can just "show up" at the first meeting and "wing it" as the facilitator, you are taking a terrible chance. Invest some time before the first meeting and guarantee your success!

How do you start? First, you must plan ahead. This means addressing the basics of any meeting:

- **Where** will it held?
- **When** will it held?
- **Who** will attend?
- **What** will be the issue?

These four questions are best answered by discussing them with the leader (see the Chapter 11, "You and the Leader").

Second, you must notify the participants Written notification is the best. Sending an email note is sufficient but can easily be overlooked by the recipient — or deleted. A paper letter not only stands out but is harder to lose than its electronic cousin. And paper announcements can be done in color which draws much more attention than a black & white format.

Third, you must prepare your flipcharts This is very important. By doing your flipcharts ahead of time, you will not only convince the group that you are a professional but you will also convey to them the concept that they are important enough for you to prepare ahead of time. And you will thank yourself during the session because the flipcharts can provide a sequence for the process that can be forgotten during a "facilitator's panic." There's nothing more embarrassing as forgetting where you are in the process — having a set of prepared flipcharts will be your lifesaver!

Finally, you must set up the room This means pulling tables into place, moving chairs, setting up flipchart stands and getting fresh pads of flipchart paper, hanging groundrule charts on the wall, and doing other things essential to making the session flow. See Chapter 12, "Pre-Meeting Logistics & The Room" for more information. As the old adage goes, "You don't get credit for the preparation but you do for the results." This is true for facilitation sessions. Very few people will see the work you do beforehand and setting up the room is something most meeting participants take for granted.

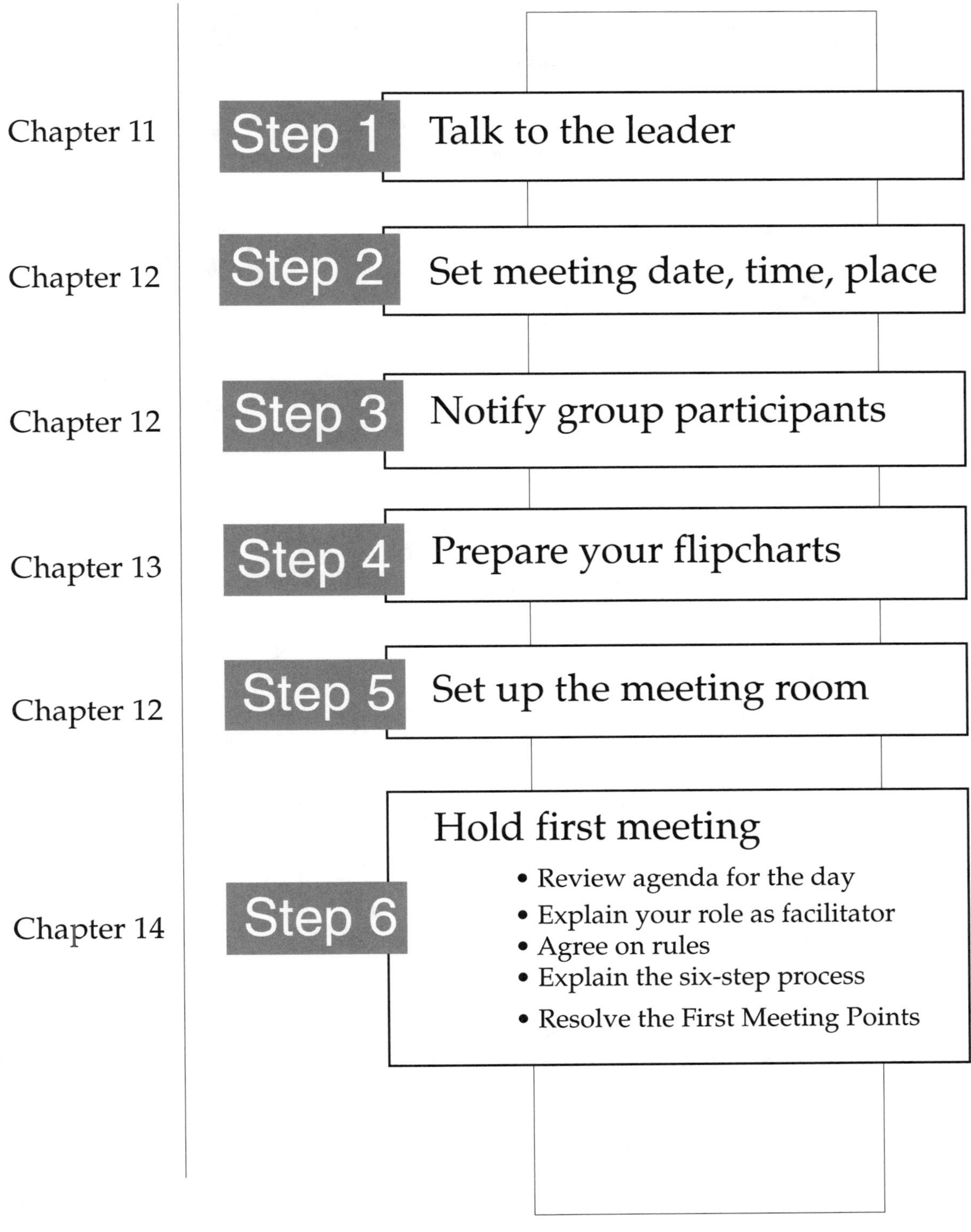
Chapter 11
Step 1
Talk to the leader
Chapter 12
Step 2
Set meeting date, time, place
Chapter 12
Step 3
Notify group participants
Chapter 13
Step 4
Prepare your flipcharts
Chapter 12
Step 5
Set up the meeting room
Chapter 14
Step 6
Hold first meeting
• Review agenda for the day
• Explain your role as facilitator
• Agree on rules
• Explain the six-step process
• Resolve the First Meeting Points

Roadmap to the First Meeting

STAKEHOLDERS

Who are these people? Stakeholders are people who have an interest in the group's output. These individuals can have anywhere from a responsibility to report on your actions to a direct impact on what the group does.

WARNING: Stake holders can derail a process. They can undermine or sabotage a group's final product. They can also create enough havoc within an organization to damage the group's effectiveness or it's credibility.

Stakeholders could be people such as:

- other employees or internal customers
- external customers or clients
- the community
- regulatory agencies
- suppliers
- special interest groups or lobbyists

Be careful and never ignore stakeholders! Part of getting started in a facilitation process is determining who are the stakeholders for the issue being worked.

Identifying the stakeholders Each issue has different stakeholders. Some will be obvious to you, such as the office manager, site supervisor, principal. Some stakeholders will be less obvious and require some probing to uncover them. Sources for identifying stakeholders are:

- the *leader* (ask her or him before the first meeting)
- the *group* (ask them during the first meeting)
- informal discussions with *other people* in the organization

Over the years a few interesting names have been substituted for stakeholders. These include favorites like "duck hunters" or "reed people" (they wait in the bushes to pop out and shoot down your ideas or actions), "bushwhackers," and the benign label of "interested parties." Look for stakeholders in any of these camps.

Both participants and stakeholders have a vested interest in the group's output. The difference is that stakeholders are usually not involved in the detailed facilitation process. So how do you keep stakeholders involved and "up to speed" with group activity?

"When you think you're over-communicating, then you're probably communicating just enough."

Keeping stakeholders involved There is a useful guideline that says, "When you think you're over-communicating, then you're probably communicating just enough." The key to keeping stakeholder involved is communicating with them. Use memos, emails, newsletters, ten-minute briefings, informal updates in the hallway, voicemail messages, or lunch meetings to keep the stakeholders abreast of group progress. If they aren't kept current on what the group is doing, then they might feel it necessary to intervene after the process is over. Do it.

This is a very important issue to resolve at the *first* meeting (see Chapter 14). Stakeholders can undo any progress made by the team. Recommendations can be *ignored* by stakeholders. Decisions can be *reversed* by them. Actions can be *cancelled* by them.

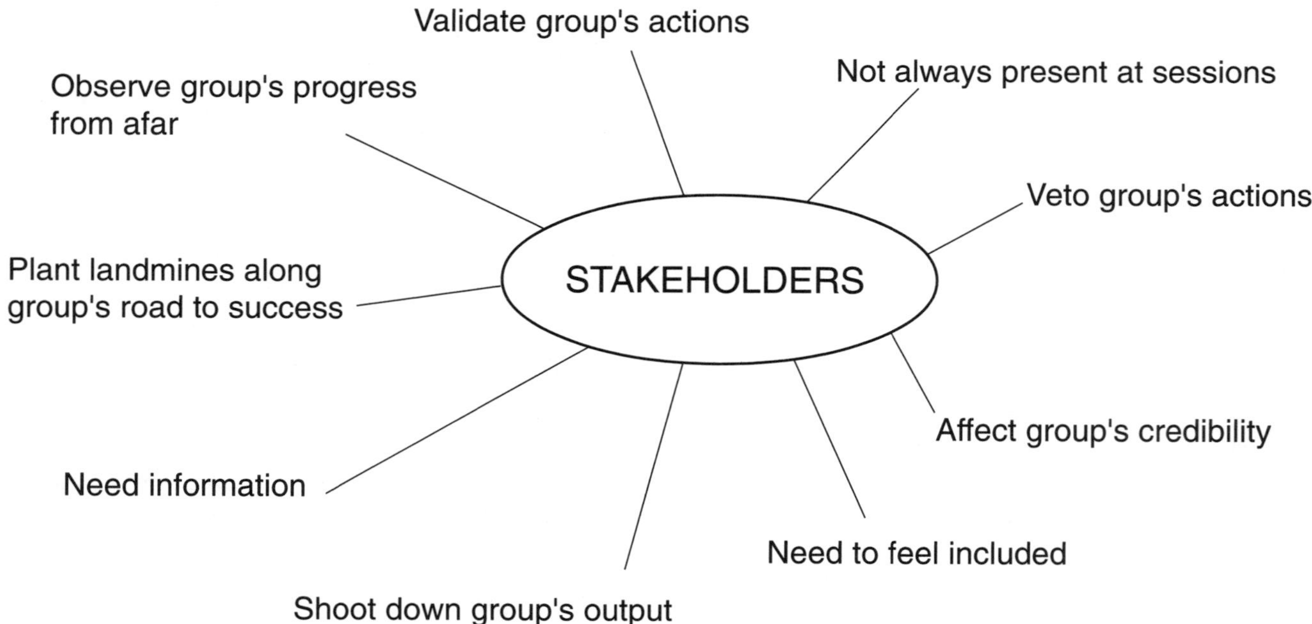

Review

Get started by doing these steps:

1. Talk to the leader
2. Set meeting date, time, place
3. Notify group participants
4. Prepare your flipcharts
5. Set up the meeting room
6. Hold first meeting

And remember...

Stakeholders: individuals that are...

- Responsible for final decisions
  OR
- Affected by those decisions
  OR
- Have power to block those decisions

A solution to the problem of stakeholders is to *include them* in the process. If that is not possible, then the group must implement and use some kind of *communication link* with them. Such communication will keep the stakeholders abreast of group actions and decisions... and avoid unpleasant surprises to either group.

"I can live two months on a good compliment."
— **Mark Twain**

> "I must follow them. I am their leader."
> — **Andrew Bonar Law,**
> *Conservative Prime Minister, 1922-1923*

11 YOU AND THE LEADER

There is a leader We occasionally forget that there is someone else that plays a major role in facilitating a group. That person (or persons) is the leader.

Historically, groups have attempted to make decisions with the leader as the meeting facilitator. It is very natural for a supervisor to call a meeting of her or his direct reports in order to resolve some issue. The difficulties of having such an imbalance of power (and consequences) around the table are obvious.

Your relationship with the leader One of the benefits of facilitated decision-making is that the facilitator is neutral. But there is a very important relationship between the facilitator and the leader. The facilitator will ask the leader for some specific empowerment to manage the process during the meeting. And the leader will expect the facilitator, while remaining neutral to the issue, to achieve some specific results.

Facilitator

Leader

Group

This relationship is important and should not be understated as a key relationship during the process.

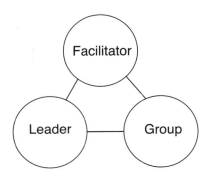

The leader is someone who has initiated this process by asking for a facilitator (you) to help his or her group address some issue.

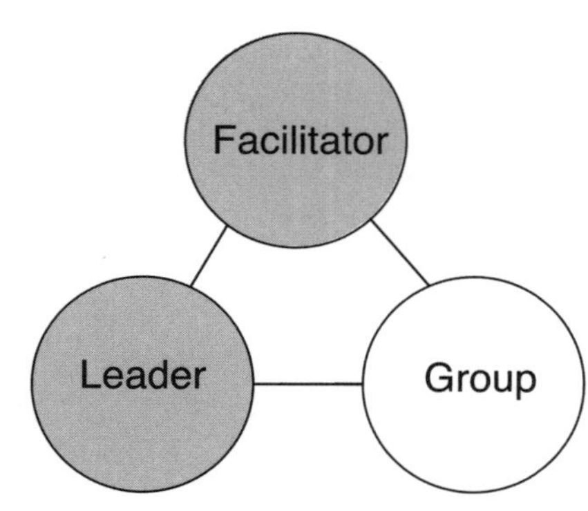

It is very important that you as the facilitator and the leader have a clear understanding and agreement regarding (1) the process, (2) the roles/relationships of the group, the facilitator, & leader, and (3) the leader's expectations of this facilitative process.

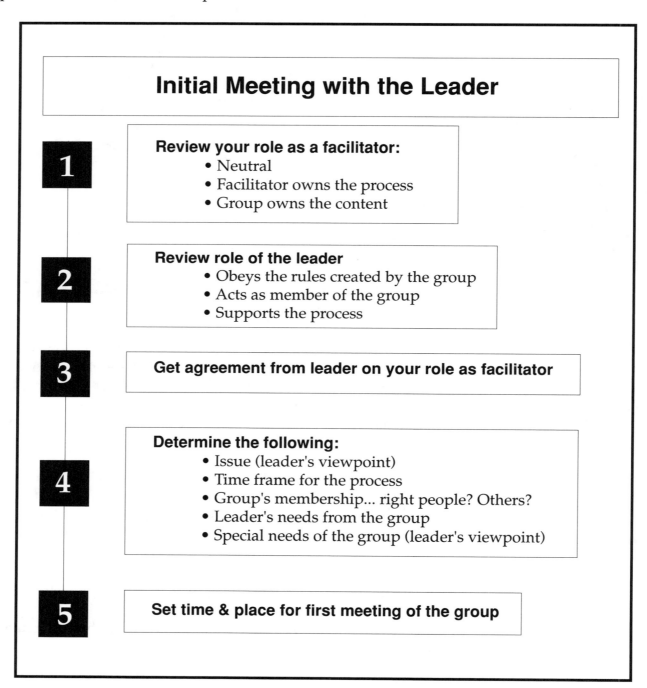

Initial Meeting with the Leader

1. **Review your role as a facilitator:**
   - Neutral
   - Facilitator owns the process
   - Group owns the content

2. **Review role of the leader**
   - Obeys the rules created by the group
   - Acts as member of the group
   - Supports the process

3. **Get agreement from leader on your role as facilitator**

4. **Determine the following:**
   - Issue (leader's viewpoint)
   - Time frame for the process
   - Group's membership... right people? Others?
   - Leader's needs from the group
   - Special needs of the group (leader's viewpoint)

5. **Set time & place for first meeting of the group**

WORKSHEET

Directions: Photocopy this worksheet. Use it during your initial meeting with the leader. Use the information you collect to plan your first meeting with the group.

1. Who is the leader(s)?

2. What is the leader's objective in working a facilitative process with the group?

3. What is the leader's idea of the "issue statement" for the group?

4. Some key elements or points that the leader would like covered as part of the process...

5. Time frame?

- Start:
- End process:
- "drop-dead" deadline:

6. Members of the group...

7. Other people that maybe should be part of the group...

8. Special needs of the leader....

9. Special needs of the group...

10. Leader's opinion on:

- Meeting frequency
- Meeting location
- Meeting day & time

Source: "*Facilitation Skills: Helping Groups Make Decisions*. Gregory B. Putz, Deep Space Technology Company, 2002. ISBN 0-9664456-1-9.

What's the
AUTHORITY LEVEL of the GROUP?

Authority Rating

+++

D = DECIDE

You have the authority to decide.

++

C = CONSULT

You have the responsibility to give advice.

+

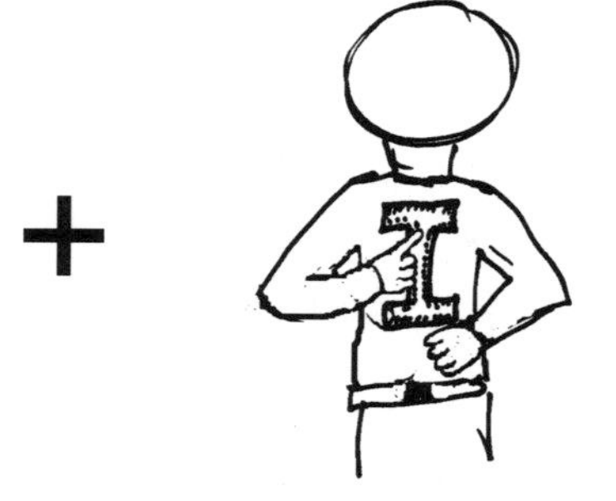

I = INFORM

You receive information or give information.

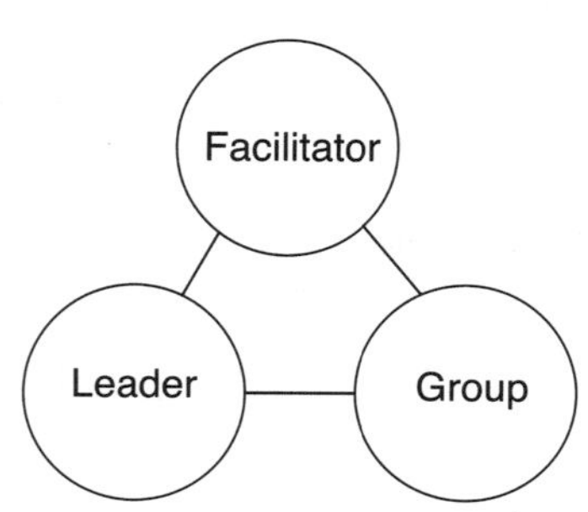

It is your responsibility to make clear at the first meeting the group's authority level.

How to explain the

AUTHORITY LEVEL of the GROUP

You have the "D"

The team's job is to decide on action. The group has the authority to commit personnel, money, and other resources to getting something done. Having the "D" means the group has the highest authority to getting things done.

You have the "C"

The team has the role of giving advice. The group may suggest action, alternatives, or possibilities - with the clear understanding that someone else will decide the action to be taken. Having the "C" means the group has the resources and credibility to advise others on action to be taken.

You have the "I"

The team is formed to listen and speak. The group is not expected to make recommendation or take action. It is created only to receive or give information.

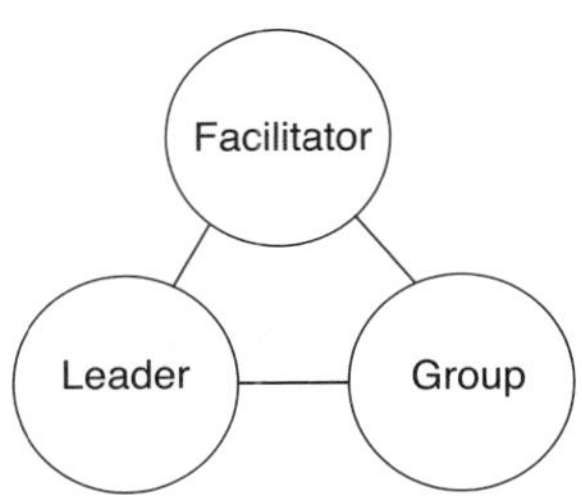

AUTHORITY LEVEL examples

DECIDE

- Teams that implement business strategies
- Groups that build or install things
- Groups that are relatively independent & have a good "track record" of accomplishments

CONSULT

- Incident investigation teams
- Ad hoc committees
- Fact-finding teams/blue-ribbon panels
- Research teams
- Benchmarking teams

INFORM

- Department meetings (mainly sharing information)
- Town hall meetings (sharing and gathering opinions)
- Focus groups/survey teams

The PROBLEM

Groups don't know their authority level. They decide on action that is later "shot down" by higher authorities. The result is anger and distrust.

The SOLUTION

Make clear the group's authority level (D? C? I?) at the *first* meeting. *Remember, this level is set by the leader and not by the group.*

Review

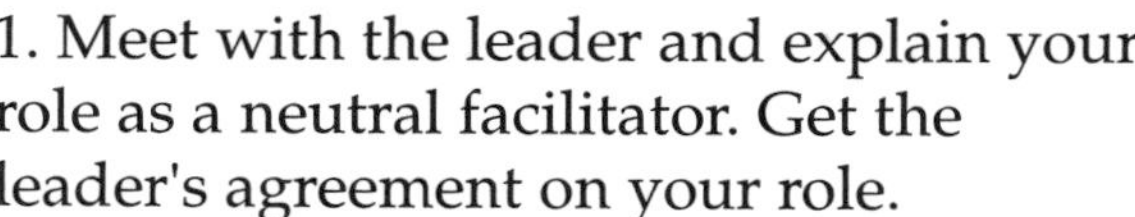

1. Meet with the leader and explain your role as a neutral facilitator. Get the leader's agreement on your role.

2. Review the leader's role in the facilitation process. Get the leader's agreement on his or her role.

3. Agree with the leader on the details of the process (issue, timing, names of participants, authority level of the group).

4. Find out if the leader has any special needs. Agree on "what success looks like" for this issue and process.

5. Remember that a group has three possible levels of authority: decision (D), consulting (C), or information (I).

And remember...

- The leader is your prime customer in this process. It is important that you maintain an open line of communications with the leader throughout the process.

- Don't let the leader overpower the group during the facilitation process.

- Feel free to contact other stakeholders during the process to communicate the group's progress.

"Management problems always turn out to be people problems."
— **John Peet**

> "No one gets credit for being prepared... they only get credit for getting results."
>
> — **Old Saying**

12 PRE-MEETING LOGISTICS & THE ROOM

A positive start Here is your opportunity to get the facilitation process off to a good start. Before you move ahead, do four things:

- First, you must **set the date, time, & place** of the meeting.
- Second, you must **reserve the room**.
- Third, you must **notify** the participants.
- Fourth, you must **set up** the room

The first two items can be directly accomplished. The third, notifying the participants, should follow the format shown in this chapter. The fourth item, setting up the room, is critical to creating a positive impact on the participants.

Additional work In addition to these four tasks, another important one is preparing the flipcharts and posters. Doing this before the session will free the facilitator to welcome the participants and create a cordial atmosphere in the meeting.

Example of pre-meeting "Welcome Letter"

- **Identify the leader(or sponsor) of this activity.**
- **What are the benefits of doing this?**
- **When & where?**
- **Identify any pre- work.**
- **Questions?**
- **Positive reinforce-ment for participating!**

M E M O R A N D U M

Bountiful, UT
November 24

Night Crew -
Group Facilitation

Caroline,
Our supervisor, Suzie, has asked that your work team **solve a problem** regarding cost accounting of damaged merchandise. She has **asked me to facilitate** a seried of problem-solving meetings with the night crew.

The **benefits** of solving this problem are:

- lower operating costs
- fewer injuries
- increased break time for crew members

We will hold **our first meeting** at 10:00 a.m. on this coming December 26 in the company conference room.

Before the meeting, please review the attached company policy on damaged merchandise and **be prepared to brainstorm possible solutions**. I will be a neutral facilitator during these meetings and my goal is to help the group identify needed action items to solve this problem.

Please call me at 123-4567 if I can answer any questions regarding the meeting objectives or the facilitation process.

Thank you for helping the night crew solve this problem!

Danielle

attachments
cc: Suzie

Importance of the Welcome Letter

THE ROOM

2 hours

Two hours is the optimal time for a facilitated, problem-solving meeting.

During those two hours, participants will remain in a room that can either help or hurt the process. Your responsibility as a facilitator is to prepare the room so that it conveys a positive atmosphere to the proceeding.

This is one of the most frequently overlooked steps in a successful facilitation. On the next page are some suggestions on how to make the room help you... and also help the group be more effective during their problem-solving meeting.

Warning: Always take the time (about 30 minutes) before the meeting to arrange the room. Plan to come early and leave late at every facilitation you undertake.

"The world is divided into people who do things - and people who get the credit."

— **Dwight Morrow**

How the room looks to the group...

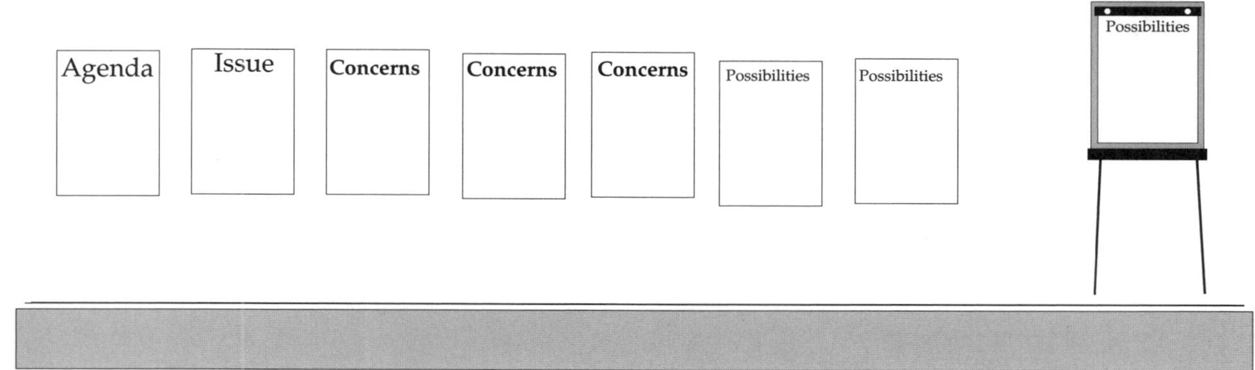

SUGGESTIONS:

- Stand in front of group
- Use a flipchart easel
- Hang flipchart sheets in front of group
- The more bright lighting the better!

How the room looks from overhead...

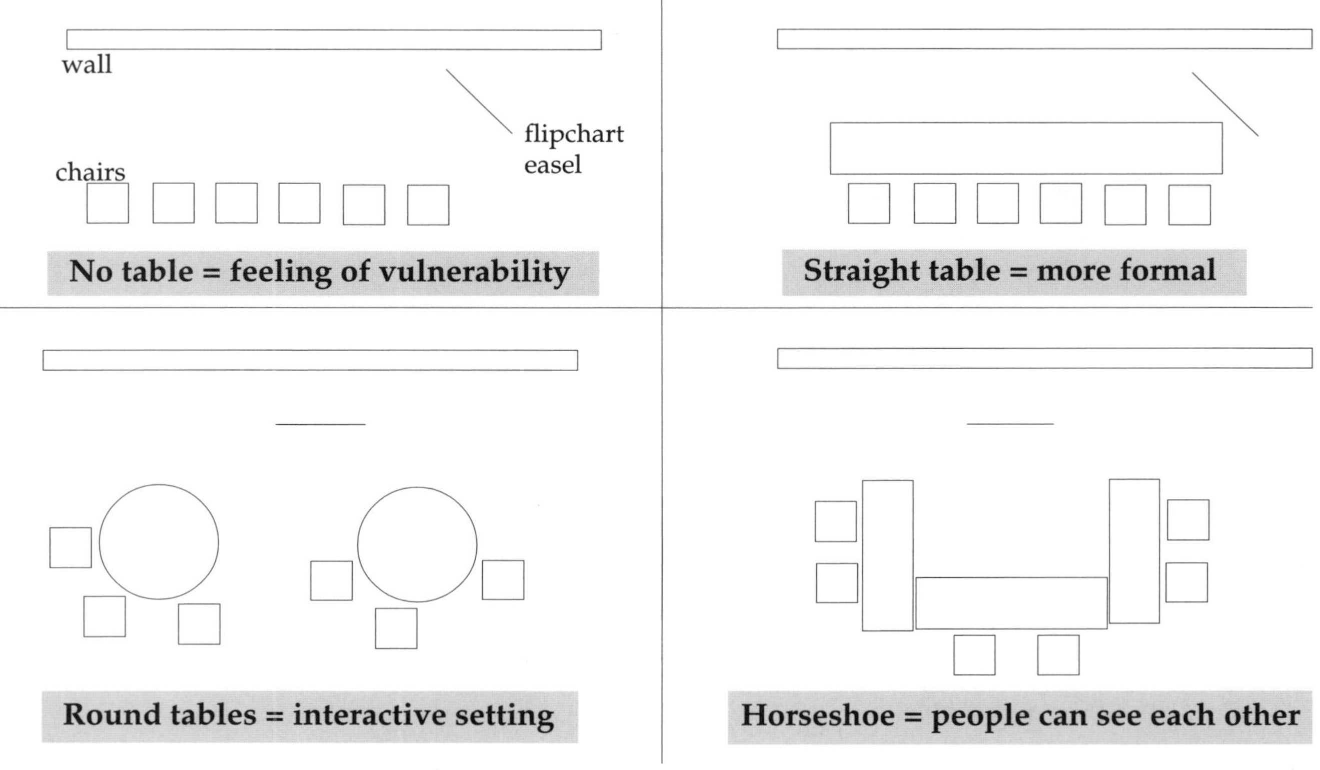

Suggested room setup...

"The proof of the pudding is in the eating."
- **Miguel de Cervantes**
from *Don Quixote de la Mancha*

Review

- Reserve the room
- Send out welcome letters
- Prepare the room before participants arrive
- Use color and lights to create an exciting atmosphere
- Use food as positive reinforcement for attending

And remember...

• You never get credit for preparation but you do for results. Make the extra effort to send out a welcome letter that explains the purpose of the session, benefits to the participants, and the time, location, and date of the event

• If you look unprepared then participants will have doubts about your ability to facilitate. Having tables, posters, flipchart easels, and supplies (paper, pencils, note pads) in place will create a positive first impression.

"The way to succeed is to double your failure rate."
— **Thomas J. Watson**

> "Man is a tool-using animal... Without tools he is nothing, with tools he is all."
>
> — **Thomas Carlyle**

13 FLIPCHARTS AND OTHER VISUAL TOOLS

Why visual tools? Human beings are visual animals and function better when ideas and concepts are graphically shown to them. Since the facilitator owns the process, the appropriate tools are needed to maintain a *visual format* for the group. Research has shown that people remember more if they see it. We remember:

10 % of what we read
20% of what we hear
30% of what we **see**
50% of what we **see and hear**

Your visual tools With experience you will repeatedly depend on same tools: flipcharts, pens, Post-It™ notes, masking tape. If you conduct formal facilitations long enough, you probably will assemble a *toolkit* containing these items (except the flipcharts). Having such a toolkit is useful since most successful facilitators routinely prepare their flipcharts, wallcharts, and other visual aids beforehand. Learning to select and use the correct tools will not only save you time, but will also enhance the group's perception of your facilitation skills.

Types of Visual Tools

Posters Use flipchart sheets to create posters for your room. Posters should be colorful and graphic. They attract participants' attention throughout the session and are valuable in communicating important concepts.

Lists Prepare lists to get ideas flowing. Large, hand-drawn flipcharts in contrasting colors are best. Use the correct colors (example: blue to stimulate creative thinking, red to shown emphasis, purple to inspire). Avoid yellows and oranges since they are hard to read.

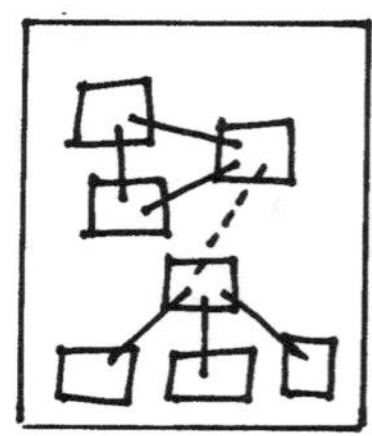

Cluster Diagrams Show circles, groups, clouds, and other geometric shapes to invite comparisons. Use radial lines, angles, and dotted lines to focus the participants' attention. Draw big!

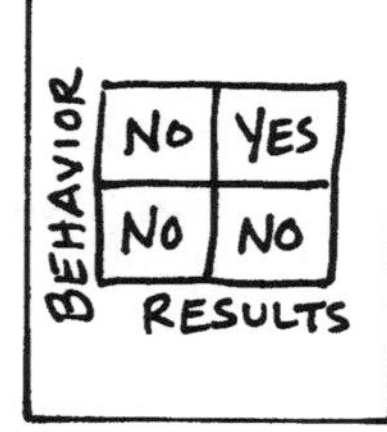

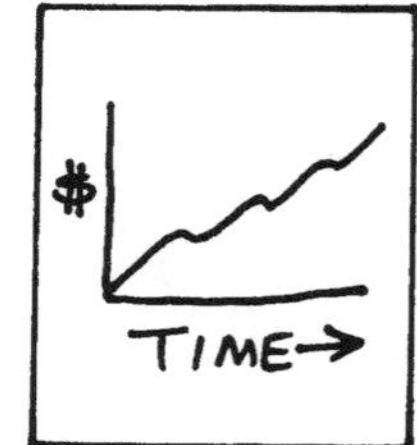

Grids Matrices and boxes show logical relationships. Graphics show trends. Make sure that you label the columns and rows clearly. Grids make excellent templates that the facilitator can fill in during the session.

Drawings Use cartoons, figures, shapes, and symbols to make humorous drawings. Familiar scenes of the workplace are comfortable and allow the participant to relate to important concepts and ideas.

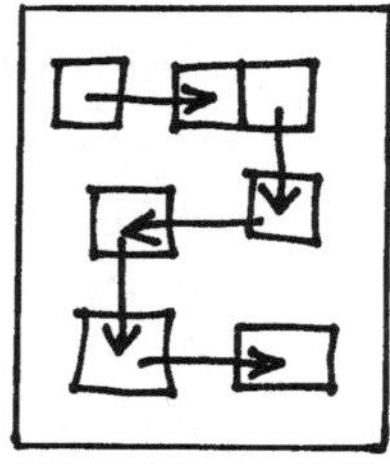

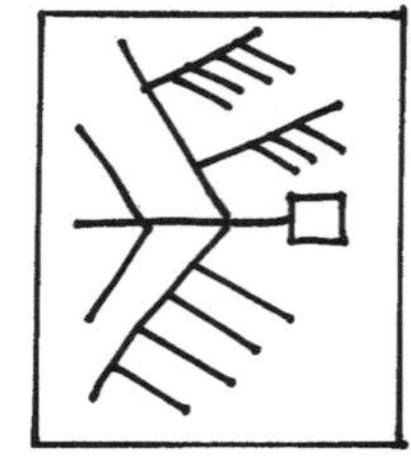

Diagrams Geometric shapes with links and arrows can be used to show logical flow of events, ideas, or timing. Diagrams do an excellent job of graphically representing linear and branching relationships.

Facilitator's Toolkit

- Tape, 3/4" transparent
- Tape, masking, 1" wide
- Tape, white, correction type, 1" wide
- Dots, adhesive, 3/4" diameter, colored
- Scissors
- Marking Pens, chisel (broad) point
- 3M Post-It™ notes
- Ruler, 18"
- Paper clips
- Pencil (preferably blue)
- Flipchart easel
- Flipchart pads (1" square grids)
- Watch or clock
- Smile, big one

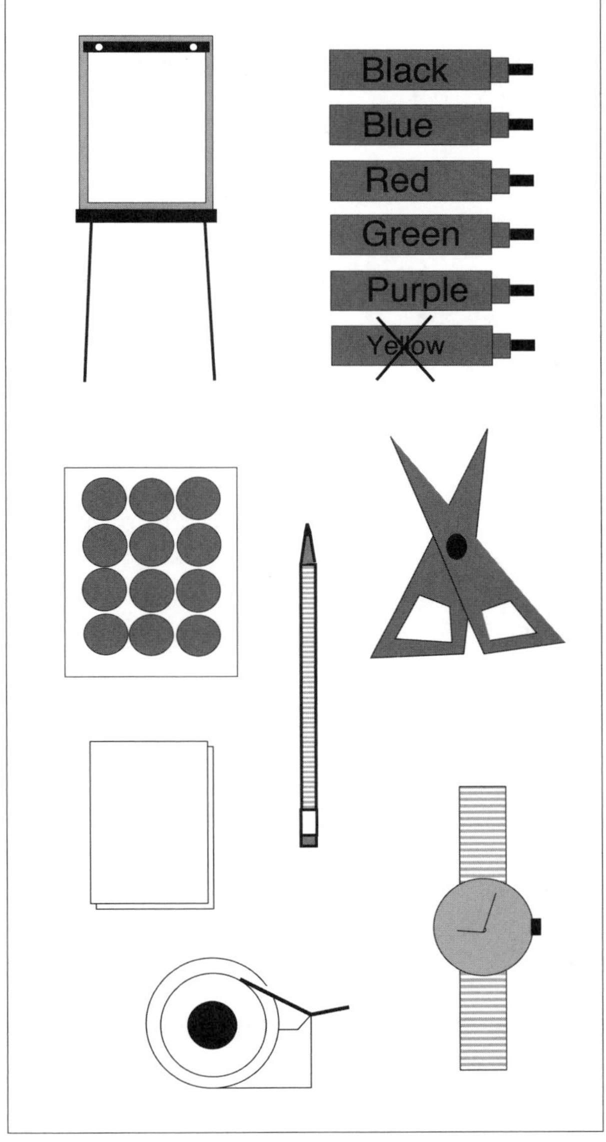

TIP **Your large pens should be a water-base type and not the solvent or alcohol-base type. Why? Because the solvent pens bleed through the paper and mark the next flipchart. And the smell really gets to you after writing with them!**

TIP **Make a mistake while writing on the flipchart? Just use the 1" white correction tape and cover it up! It's neat and you can just write directly on the tape... and the group won't be able to tell the difference!**

Colors Create Passion

Color	Impact on Group	Best Use on Flipchart
Blue	Creativity	• Text Lettering • Backgrounds
Violet	Sophisticated	• Lettering
Red	Stimulation	• Warnings/Notices • Borders • Highlights • Accents
Orange	Excitement	• Border • Highlights
Yellow	Cheerful	• Highlights
Green	Restful	• Borders • Accents
Brown	Sensible	• Drawings
Black	Decisive	• Lettering
Pink	Romantic	• Highlights

YOU WANT TO COME TO OUR FACILITATION SESSION? WE NEED THE COLOR!

How boring is the repetitive use of a black pen on a white flipchart! Often we forget that people like colors. Drab, monotonous black marker pens are too common in facilitation sessions! Why not add some spice to your session use some colors?

Research has shown that different colors create different responses in people. Let's look at some colors and their effect on people.

Blue is the most favorite color. Blue relaxes people. The absence of red makes it less tiring than the warmer violet. More importantly, blue sparks creativity in people. *Use blue backgrounds or blue lettering in your flipcharts when collecting concerns or brainstorming.* Never use blue when writing warning or cautionary statements.

Violet, the reddish sister of blue, is the most restful color. Violet creates the aura of power and self-confidence. Whereas blue triggers creativity in people, violet is more relaxing. Clinical research shows that it reduces blood pressure, pulse and respiration rates. But be careful! Large solid blocks of violet can be overwhelming so use it only for lettering and not as backgrounds in large areas.

Red is the most stimulating color. Red increases blood pressure, pulse and respiration rates. Red is the color to use when an exclamatory title is needed on a flipchart. Cautions, warnings, and other "participant-beware" statements should be written in large, red letters. *Warning: writing in red can be hard to see for most people, so always use letters at least three inches tall when using a red marker pen.* Interestingly enough, splashes of red can enhance creativity and the appetite of a group.

Orange, red's yellowish brother, is an exciting color. It raises your heart rate but lacks the punch of red. Because of this it is called a "cheap" color. Orange should be avoided as a color for lettering unless it is used sparingly and with very tall letters. Why? Orange is difficult to see. It lacks red's importance. If you want to deliver the message of importance then write in red! The best use for orange on flipcharts is as a border or a highlight.

Yellow is brightest and most cheerful color. It is never to be used alone for lettering unless you want to punish your group (you can't see yellow on white paper!). Yellow can raise the frustration level of a group when the color is used in large amounts. The best use for yellow is as a highlight on your flipcharts.

Green is a restful color. It lives between cheerful yellow and relaxing blue. Interestingly enough, green can inspire both excitement and passiveness. This schizophrenic nature suggests that it be used cautiously on flipcharts. This might seem like an unwarranted step, especially since most of nature is colored green, but a prudent one when facilitating groups. Green is best used for borders and accents.

Be careful when using several colors on a single flipchart page. Limit yourself to *three colors* plus black.

Graphics To Express Emotions

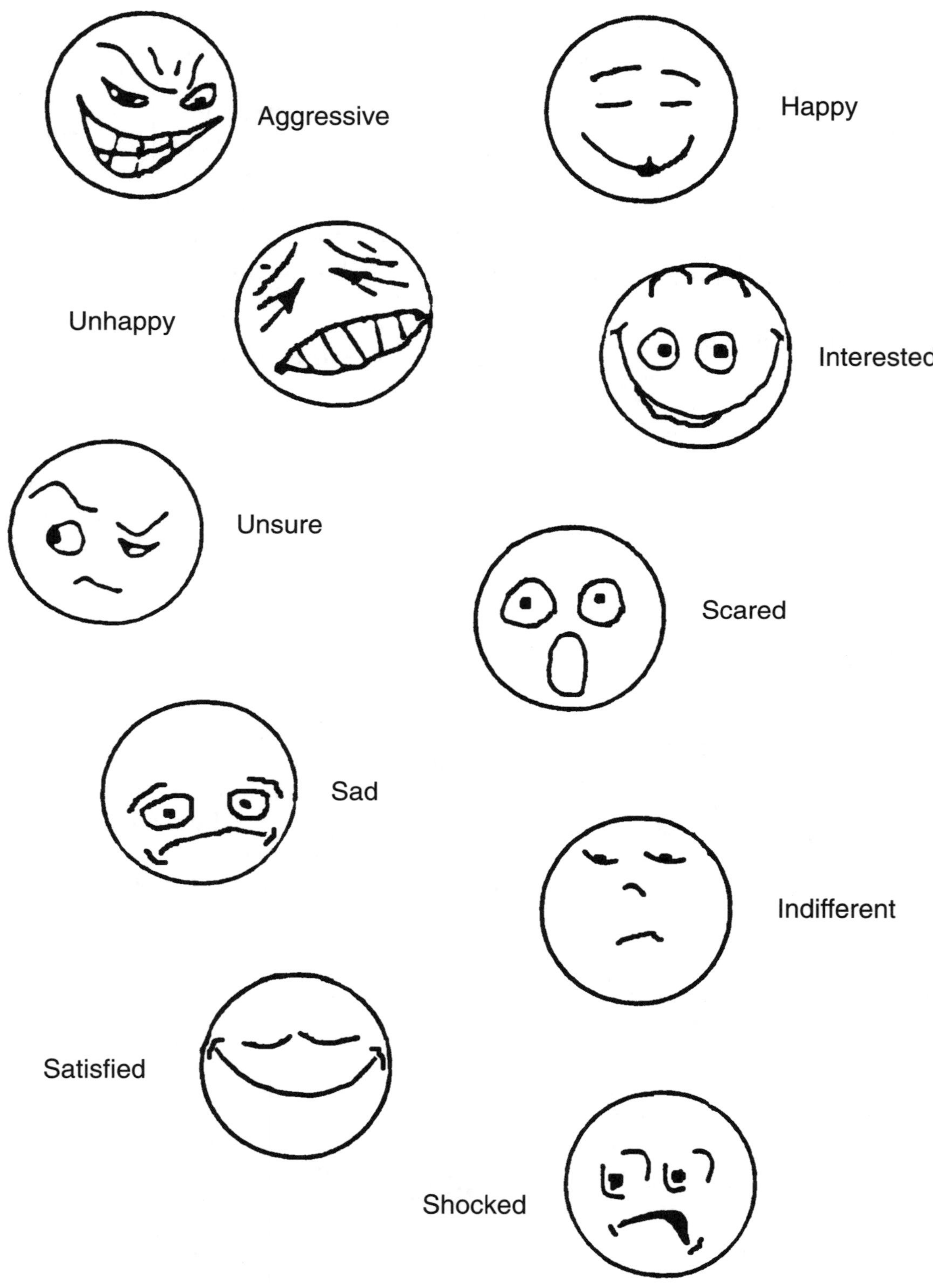

MAKE YOUR FLIPCHARTS INTERESTING !!

Use SHADOWS and accented lettering	 ABC NRA MGM ·ACTION ITEMS·
Use FIGURES	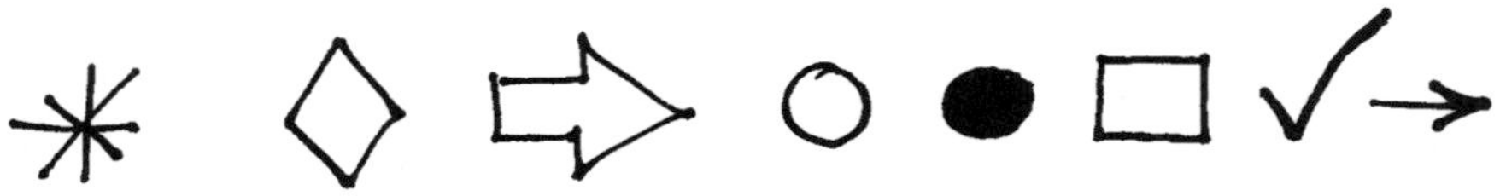
Use CARTOONS	
Use FACES and FIGURES	
Use ARROWS and FORMULAS	PLAY → FUN WORK = MONEY INVITATION → BOSS ↑ PROFITS ↓ COSTS YOU + ME = TEAM
Show SEQUENCES and ORDERS	A. B. C. 1. 2. 3. FIRST → SECOND → THIRD → TODAY: TOMORROW: NEXT MONTH:

Flipchart Management

(A) USE 2 OR MORE FLIPCHART EASELS...
AGENDA
-PROCESS-
ISSUE BIN
ROLL
(B) WHEN TURNING PAGES, ROLL THE SHEET OVER...
-I GRAB THE LOWER CORNER OF THE PAGE!
1/2"
① TEAR
② PULL
(C) TO TEAR OFF A SHEET, FIRST RIP 1/2" ALONG PERFORATION AND THEN PULL DOWN AT AN ANGLE...

Flipchart Hints & Tips

Flipchart guidelines Put the flipchart where everyone can see it. The best location is directly beneath a ceiling light — the extra illumination will make the colors "jump out" at the group. Use flipchart paper with faint one-inch by one-inch grids to help you write in level manner. And always use water-based color pens. They don't soak through the paper and smell (whew!) like the alcohol-based marker pens. The best flipchart pens are the scented watercolor markers.

Lettering Always write in LARGE block letters at least one and one-half inches tall. Two inches tall is better. Skip a line between entries and never write in red or orange unless the letters are over three inches tall (it is difficult for people to distinguish letters in these colors at a distance). Never write in yellow (unless you want to punish the group).

Pages Leave a blank flipchart page between the ones you write on. Even the best flipchart paper is semi-transparent and the writing on the underneath page will show if you don't leave a blank page between it and the page above it.

Where you stand Like the old saying goes, "You make a better door than a window." So try to stand to one side of the flipchart while writing. And don't fall into the trap of talking while you write — people cannot hear you when you are facing the easel. Write quickly and minimize the time you have your back to the group.

Highlighting Use circles, boxes, underlining, arrows, contrasting colors, pictures, smiley faces, and cartoons to highlight key words and concepts. Participants will focus faster and remember better. Have some fun!

Abbreviate Spelling isn't important for facilitators. Avoid this problem and abbreviate as much as you can. If the group doesn't understand your abbreviation, they will tell you. You'll save time and worry about spelling.

The Recorder

The Recorder If you are fortunate, you will have the services of a scribe or recorder to help you. The recorder is your assistant and should not be a participant. The role of the recorder is to write the group's ideas and comments on the flipcharts while you are free to facilitate the process. The recorder supports the facilitator and remains neutral.

Characteristics The recorder must have legible handwriting, be comfortable standing at the flipchart easel, and be quick enough to keep up with the flow of information. The latter skills requires a sense of capturing the essence of each comment and recording it accurately. The recorder has the power to stop and ask for clarification if confused.

Helping the recorder The facilitator has the responsibility to help the recorder by pacing the group and repeating information (to the recorder) while he or she writes. This includes monitoring the recorder's success and assisting whenever needed.

Other help To help the recorder, the facilitator may also ask one or more participants to help tape or hang completed flipchart sheets on the wall. This assistance will greatly help the pace of the session and free the recorder to continue writing after a flipchart page is full.

Warning Avoid selecting someone from the group to be the recorder. Otherwise, this "lucky" participant who has to act as recorder loses a great deal of opportunity to contribute. If a participant must act as recorder for the group (for example, the facilitator has an injured hand and cannot write) then ample opportunity must be given to the person to contribute her or his ideas.

On every flipchart sheet, ALWAYS write two things: (1) the DATE, and (2) the PAGE NUMBER of the sheet. Do this without exception!

Review

Flipcharts & Visual Tools

- Write BIG
- Use posters, lists, clusters, grids, drawings, and diagrams
- Abbreviate
- Leave a blank flipchart between pages
- Colors create emotions — pick the right ones!

And remember...

- Minimize the time you spend with your back to the group.
- Spelling doesn't count — but accuracy and speed does!
- Use more than one flipchart to make your job easier.
- If you can, get a recorder (scribe) to help you record ideas.
- Prepare beforehand as many flipcharts as possible.

"Enthusiasm is that kindling spark which marks the difference between the leaders in every activity and the laggards who put in just enough to get by."
— **Johann Friedrich Schiller**

> "A ship in harbor is safe, but that is not what ships are built for."
>
> — **John A. Shedd**

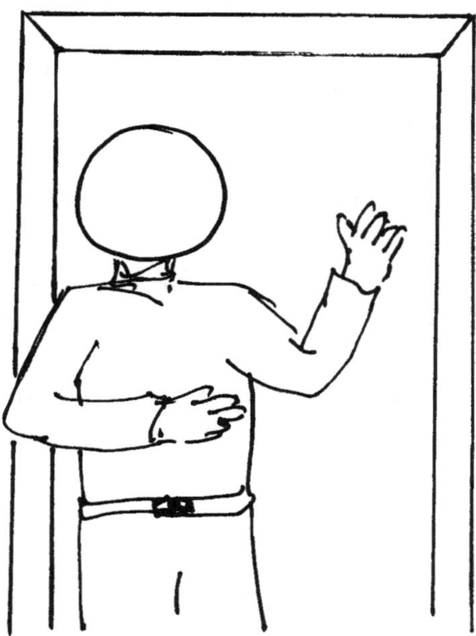

14 THE FIRST MEETING

The day has arrived for your first group meeting. Everyone is nervous. Everyone is unsure of what's expected. You're in the center spotlight. Ready to go?

Rule 1 There are five steps to follow in the *first* meeting:

- #1 - Review the agenda
- #2 - Explain your role
- #3 - Agree on rules of conduct
- #4 - Explain the six-step problem-solving process
- #5 - Resolve some important issues called "The First Meeting Points"

Rule 2 Schedule the meeting for two hours. After two hours, stop. You'll need a break... and the group will need time to think over the issues and materials reviewed.

Rule 3 And don't forget to schedule the *second* meeting before everyone leaves the meeting room!

Rule 4 Be positive and enthusiastic!

Why do first meetings fail?

Reasons for troubled first meetings Experience has shown that the first meeting is most critical one of the facilitation process. Why? Listed below are some reasons why first meetings don't go as smoothly as desired.

- Hesitant participation by group members.
- Some participants are impatient and refuse to invest their time in the process.
- Participants have reservations about expressing their innermost personal desires, feelings, and preferences about the issue.
- Complaints about the group's composition, meeting time, location, etc.
- Suspicion about the neutrality of the facilitator - and trust.
- Lack of interest.
- Fear of vulnerability — risk of exposure, reprisals, or revenge.

What you can do It is possible to mitigate the impact of these causes of poor first meetings. A facilitator has control over the process. And the facilitator can do specific things to help reduce the impact of these problems. Here are some suggestions:

> **Sell the benefits** Show group members how they will personally benefit from participating in this process and addressing the issue. *Do not explain the benefits to the company or organization.* People want to hear their favorite radio station, WII-FM ("what's in it for me").

> **Build trust** Reassure the group, repeatedly, about your neutral role. Then behave like a trusted, neutral facilitator.

> **Create excitement** Get excited in front of the group and explain why working on this issue is the BEST thing that ever happened to the company and each of them. Excitement is contagious. Try it.

Step 1

Hold first meeting

- Review agenda for the day
- Explain your role as facilitator
- Agree on rules
- Explain the six-step process
- Resolve the First Meeting Points

- Make the agenda *before* the meeting
- Review the agenda (aloud) with the group
- Ask the group, "Is there anything you want to add or change?" (If so... do it!)
- Finish by asking the group, "What time do we want to finish today?"

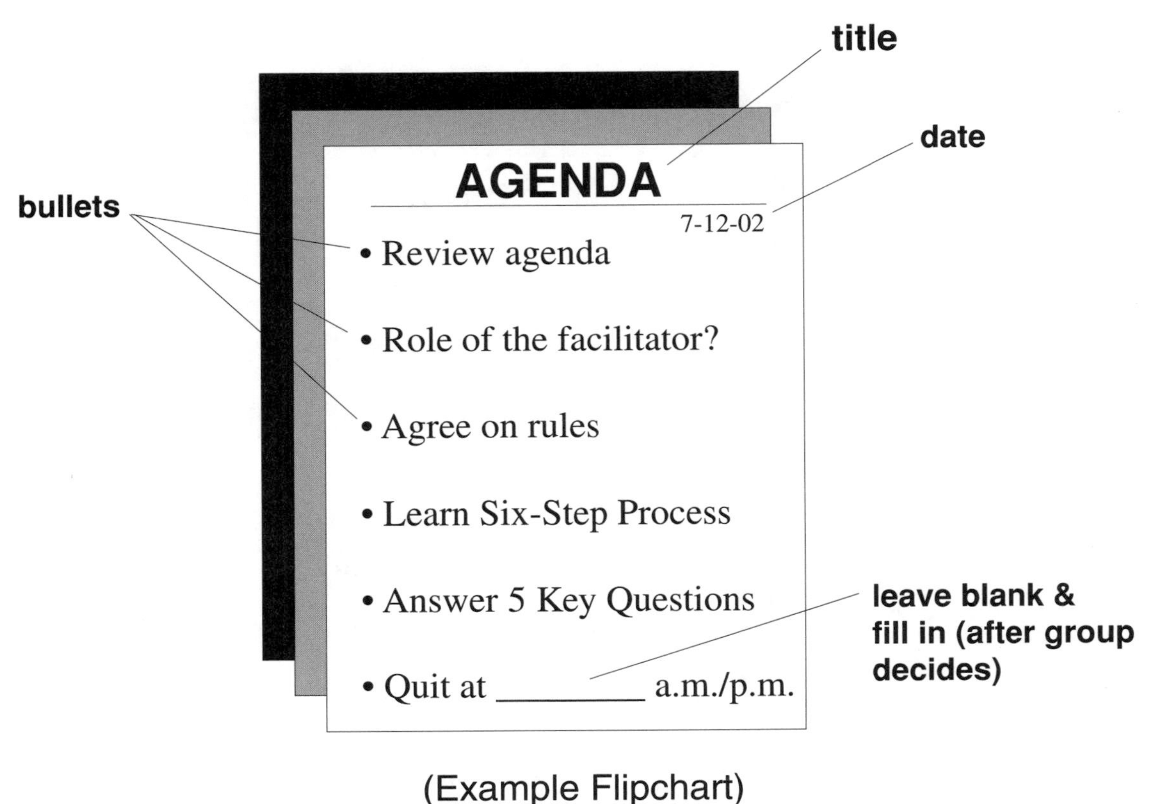
title
date
bullets
AGENDA
7-12-02
• Review agenda
• Role of the facilitator?
• Agree on rules
• Learn Six-Step Process
• Answer 5 Key Questions
• Quit at ________ a.m./p.m.
leave blank & fill in (after group decides)

(Example Flipchart)

Step 2

Hold first meeting

- Review agenda for the day
- Explain your role as facilitator
- Agree on rules
- Explain the six-step process
- Resolve the First Meeting Points

Share with the group some thoughts about your role...

- "...I'm here to *help* the group!"
- "...I'm *neutral* on this issue!"
- "...please help me... if your see me not being neutral, please *stop me* and tell me!"
- "...the group owns the *content* and I own the *process* we'll follow in this meeting."
- "...my job is to *enforce* the process and the rules."

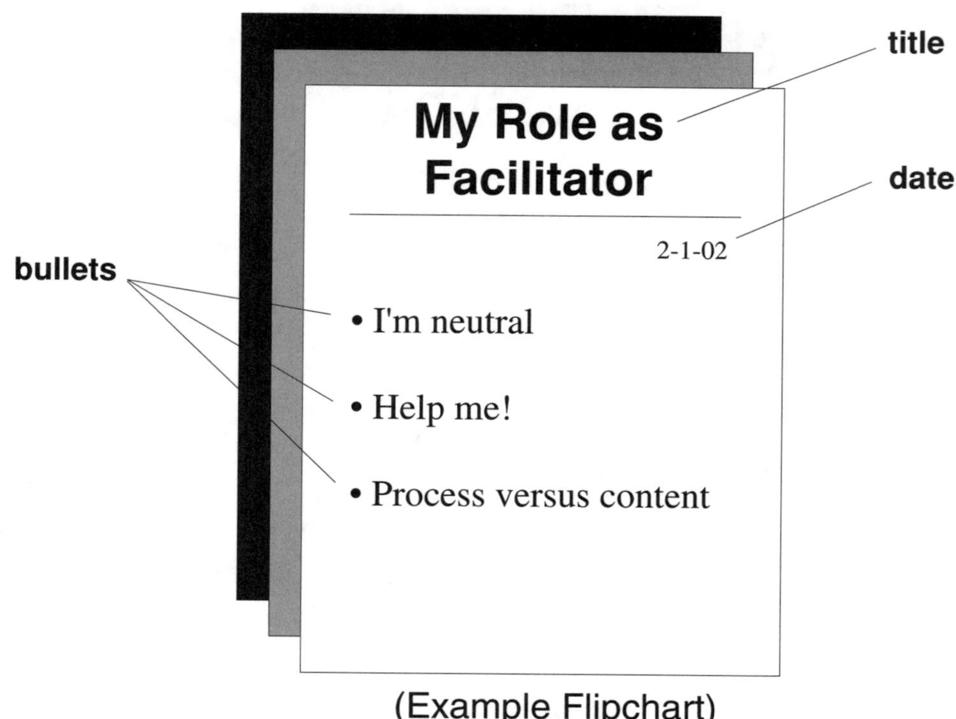
My Role as Facilitator
2-1-02
• I'm neutral
• Help me!
• Process versus content
title
date
bullets

(Example Flipchart)

- Make a flipchart of rules (before the meeting)
- Hang flipchart on wall in meeting room
- Ask the group, "Do you agree with these rules?"
- Delete, add, or change the rules as the group desires

BASIC

Step 3

Hold first meeting

- Review agenda for the day
- Explain your role as facilitator
- Agree on rules
- Explain the six-step process
- Resolve the First Meeting Points

Rules for the Group

❄ Only one person speaks at a time
❄ No side conversations
❄ Silence is acceptable
❄ No rank in the room
❄ Everyone participates
❄ No one dominates
❄ What is said stays in the room
❄ This is a "safe zone" to speak in
❄ No "grandstanding"
❄ Attack problems, not people
❄ Group will follow the process
❄ OK to question the process at any time
❄ OK to change the rules
❄ OK to change the process
❄ OK to change your mind
❄ Facilitator will enforce the rules
❄ Group will help the facilitator
❄ End on time
❄ Start on time — and no rewind!

- Make these rules on a separate flipchart
- Ask the group, "Would you like to include any of these rules, also?"

Step 3

Hold first meeting

- Review agenda for the day
- Explain your role as facilitator
- Agree on rules
- Explain the six-step process
- Resolve the First Meeting Points

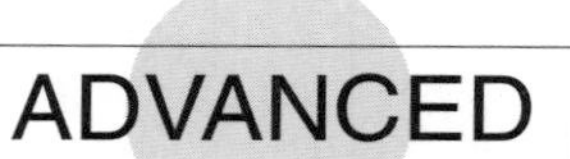

More Rules for the Group

❊ No negative responses for someone raising an issue at any time

❊ Group focuses on "true consensus" versus "driving to completion"

❊ Members don't respond defensively to questions

❊ Members use tact in asking questions — ask supportively for understanding, not aggressively

❊ Listen as an ally

❊ Give freely of your experience

❊ Keep an open mind

❊ Be an active listener

Want more examples of ground rules?
See Chapter 23, "Examples You Can Use."

Step 4

Hold first meeting

- Review agenda for the day
- Explain your role as facilitator
- Agree on rules
- Explain the six-step process
- Resolve the First Meeting Points

- Make a flipchart (before the meeting)
- Hang flipchart on wall in meeting room

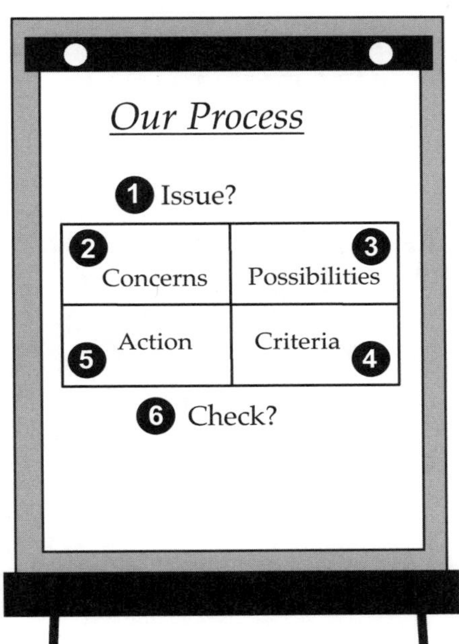

(Example Flipchart)

See the section *"Steps For Successful Facilitation"* for more information regarding the six steps of the facilitation process.

Hold first meeting

Step 5

- Review agenda for the day
- Explain your role as facilitator
- Agree on rules
- Explain the six-step process
- Resolve the First Meeting Points

At the *first* meeting, the facilitator and the group need to have an open discussion about the process. **Don't get trapped by talking about content items.** Talk about the process the group will follow to achieve resolution of the issue at hand.

A good way to come to some agreement with the group over the process steps is to discuss the five points below.

During the first meeting, help the group resolve these five points...

1 What is the scope of the task?
What is the purpose of the group? What are the problems/issues? Are there any limitations of the group? Boundaries?

2 Authority level? (D, C, or I?)
What authority does the group possess? Gather information? Recommend action? Decide and implement action?

Authority Level
See Chapter 11

3 Success looks like...
What is the goal? What will the final product look like? How will we know when we are done?

4 What process will be used?
Who are the stakeholders? How will decisions be made within the group? Consensus-based? How will the group communicate with other individuals or groups? Are the *right* people here?

Stakeholders
See Chapter 10

5 Timing?
What is expected by when? Finish by when?

C?
I?
D?
Purpose?
Boundaries?
What's our AUTHORITY?
(hint: ask the leader)
2
What's the SCOPE of our task?
1
Issue?
3
What does SUCCESS look like?
Ask the group, "Any QUESTIONS?"
FIRST MEETING
How will we know when we're done?
How much TIME do we have to finish?
Will we use consensus?
5
What's our PROCESS?
4
Are the right people here?
Who are the stakeholders?
What's our communications plan with people outside this meeting?

ISSUE BIN: A helpful tool for the first meeting

What is the benefit of an issue bin? An issue bin is a helpful tool that enables you keep the process moving. Items for the issue bins are topics or concerns that come up during the session that are not part of the agenda. Sometimes the item is a legitimate concern or concept but it is not within the scope of the group's work. It is very easy during the first meeting to get trapped in side issues or tangents. Until the group learns to work as a team and understands the process, it is common for individuals to bring up extraneous topics. Although these topics are offered with the best of intentions, they always delay timely completion of agenda items. An issue bin gives the facilitator a convenient way to acknowledge the suggestion and keep the process moving.

What goes into an issue bin? An issue bin starts with a blank flipchart sheet on the wall of the meeting room. The facilitator or scribe records the extraneous topics on this blank sheet of paper. Use the issue bin for ideas, topics or concerns:

- requiring more time than the group has available
- requiring more information
- outside the group's scope or control
- not part of the session's agenda

What happens to the issue bin? During the last stage of the facilitation process, the group will do a final check. Part of this check step is to determine what happens next. It is at this point that the facilitator should revisit the issue bin and ask the group to incorporate any of the topics in its future activities. An example would be starting a new problem-solving series using one of the issue bin subjects as the issue. Or the group could choose to incorporate one or more of the issue bin items in its action plan. In any event, the facilitator must have the group look at the issue bin one last time before ending the facilitation series.

Review

The First Meeting

- Review agenda for the day
- Explain your role as facilitator
- Agree on rules
- Explain the six-step process
- Resolve the First Meeting Points

And remember...

- Schedule the meeting for two hours.
- Schedule the *second* meeting before everyone leaves the meeting room!
- Don't forget to communicate with people outside the meeting — especially the stakeholders.
- Use an issue bin.

"I learned that a great leader is a man who has the ability to get other people to do what they don't want to do and like it."

— **Harry S. Truman**

IV

Helping You With...

15. Building **Consensus**
16. Handling **Conflict**
17. Getting **Participation**
18. Building **Trust**
19. Managing Your **Stress**

"Treat people as though they were what they ought to be and you help them become what they are capable of being."

— **Johann W. von Goethe**

> "As happy as a clam at high tide."
> — **Old Saying**

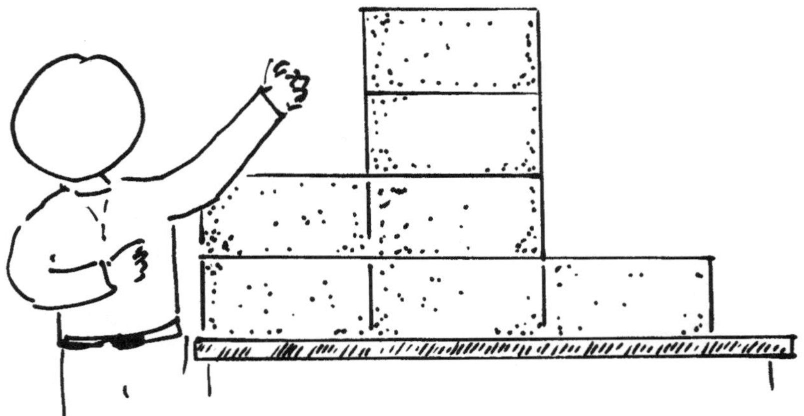

15 BUILDING CONSENSUS

Supporting the outcome Consensus requires unity but not agreement. A consensus is reached when all participants either agree with the decision or have the opportunity to be heard why not. Consensus is not a majority decision but an agreement to support the group's output. It is a useful tool that enables the group to avoid hopeless deadlocks and move ahead in the process. Conventional voting to determine agreement should be discouraged by the facilitator because it forces participants to entrench themselves in positions they later hesitate to change.

Decision choices Decisions range from leader-centered to group-centered. Leaders use authority to decide and groups use consensus. The experienced facilitator understands that the situation determines the decision style.

Satisfaction not guaranteed The goal of consensus is a decision that is consented to by all group members. Complete satisfaction by all participants is not required — in fact, it is rare. The decision must be acceptable enough that all participants will support it.

Decision Choices

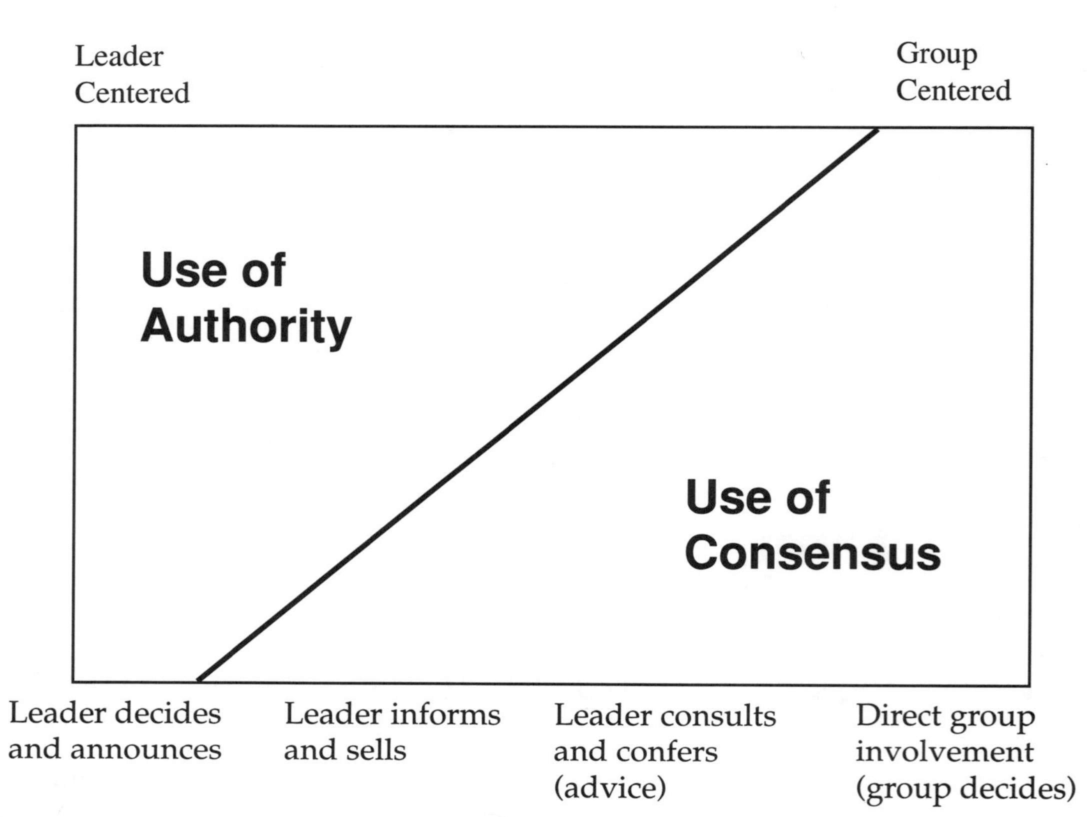

"Consensus is reached when everyone in the group can buy into, or live with, the decision without feeling compromised in any way."
-Michael Doyle & David Straus

"Consensus is when you may not agree completely with the decision, but you'll openly support it."
- Gregory Putz

ACID TEST for Consensus

The facilitator knows when a group reaches consensus when each participant can say:

- I believe that you understand my point of view
- I believe that I understand your point of view
- Whether or not I prefer this decision, I support it because it was reached openly and fairly.

Benefits of Consensus

- Decisions are more accurate
- People are more willing to support decisions
- Disagreements are explored rather than avoided
- Everyone gets a chance to be heard
- Everyone ends up with more information
- Group synergism creates a higher-quality decision

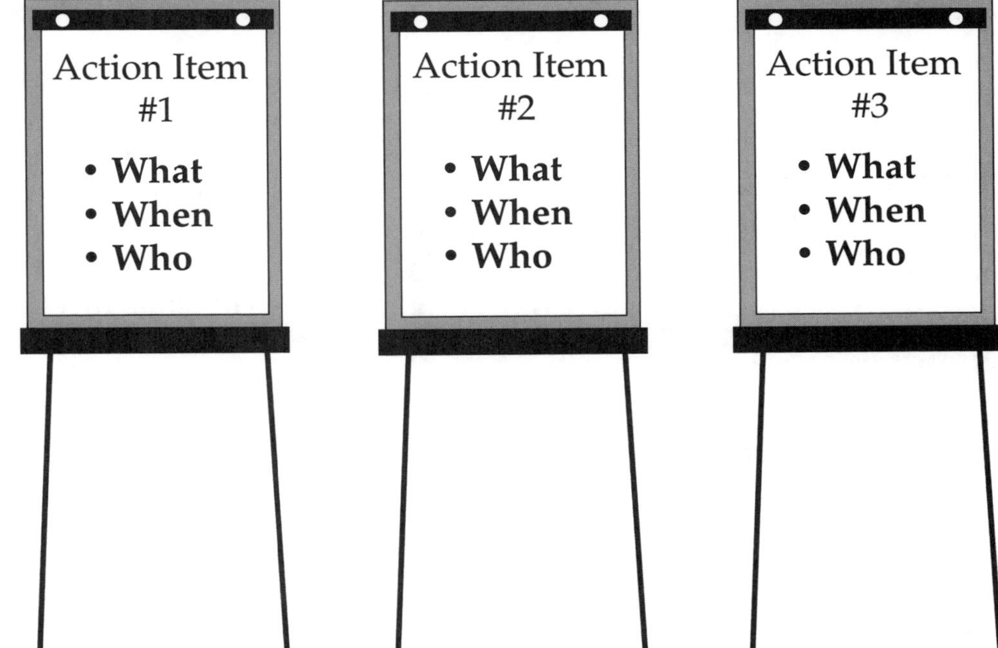

Guidelines For Reaching Consensus

For each individual

• Don't argue for your personal judgements but approach from a standpoint of logic.

• Don't change your mind just to avoid conflict and reach a speedy agreement. Look for a common ground of solutions that may not be precisely what you think is right but is close enough.

• Always remember that conflict, differences of opinion and interpretation are a helpful, strengthening attribute of consensus building.

Why not vote?

• Voting causes an individual to establish a position... and it is difficult for anyone to publicly change his or her position

• Voting ignores the opinions of the minority

• Voting avoids conflict and discussion... it denies the group the benefit of understanding others and the natural synergism created by group interaction

As the facilitator

• Make absolutely clear to the group what it is that they are seeking consensus on.

• Start off by getting the group to agree to some "lofty" or higher-purpose goal... a noble objective that they all will strive for in attempting to build a consensus.

• A certain amount of tension in the room is expected and helpful. Don't initiate any activity that prematurely smooths-over the conflict.

• Avoid any technique that reduces conflict, such as trading, voting, numerical averaging, coin-flips, or bargaining.

• Require that each individual take responsibility for hearing others and being heard... everyone participates actively and is included in building the consensus.

• Keep insisting that there be a "win/win" environment in the room. A win by the group and the individuals are more important than an solitary, individual win.

• Remind the group that conflict is good in creating consensus and is not a hinderance to it. Differences of opinion and disagreement are natural and expected.

Building Consensus

Tool Box

Negative Voting	Ask, "Can anyone <u>not</u> live with this proposal?" Ask, "Does anyone have any heartache with this...?"
Straw Voting	Say, "OK, I just want to get a feel for where we are... this is a nonbinding straw vote. How many of you can support this...?"
Win/Win	Say, "OK, it seems that you cannot support this part of the proposal... what would we have to change to make it acceptable to you?"

Use a convenient tools called "Fist or Five" to judge consensus readiness in the group. See page 15-6.

Hey ! Are you on the road to building some consensus with your group? If so, then try this little tool called...

FIST or FIVE ??

Step 1 Announce the *Fist or Five* process by say, "I want to get a feel for where the group stands on this topic. Let's take an informal, straw vote that's not binding on anyone."

Step 2 Clarify the *Fist or Five* process by explaining, "After I ask the question, I'd like everyone to indicate their current feeling about this by raising their hand with their fingers as such:

Five Fingers = YES! I agree. No more discussion! Let's move on...

Four Fingers = OK with me. I can support the group on this topic.

Three Fingers = I'm on the fence. Can we continue talking about it?

Two Fingers = I *really* don't know. I really need to talk about this a lot more.

One Finger = No. I really can't support this. We can talk, but you'll really have to convince me!

No Fingers = HECK, NO !! No way. No how. Forget it !!

Step 3 Vote and determine the average. If the average number of fingers is one, then say, "OK. The result is overwhelmingly a "one" so let's continue talking..." If the average is five, say "OK, everyone seems to support this topic, so let's move on to something else."

The biggest danger for a facilitator...

A final few words to HELP you...

1. Listen — pay attention to others
2. Encourage participation
3. Share information
4. Don't agree too quickly
5. Don't bargain or trade support
6. Don't vote
7. Treat differences as a strength
8. Create a solution that can be supported
9. Avoid arguing blindly for your own views
10. Seek a mutually beneficial solution

Building Consensus

Building Consensus

Summary

- Complete unanimity is NOT the goal.

- Discourage those who ARGUE for their position.

- Do not let the group assume that it is a win-lose situation. Encourage a WIN-WIN arrangement.

- Discourage those who change their mind simply to AVOID conflict.

- Guide the group so as to AVOID conflict-reducing techniques like voting, averaging, coin-tosses, etc.

- Be realistic - differences of opinion within the group are HEALTHY and natural; they frequently result in synergism helpful to the process.

- Do not become discouraged at the TIME REQUIRED to reach consensus; if the group becomes weary then take a break or schedule another meeting.

"Force is not a remedy."
— **John Bright,**
English liberal politician and reformer

> "Resolving conflict is rarely about who is right. It is about acknowledgment and appreciation of differences."
> — **Thomas F. Crum**, *The Magic of Conflict*

16 HANDLING CONFLICT

You cannot avoid it Conflict is natural. It is inevitable. It is not a bad thing. Conflict provides the group and the problem solving process with specific benefits:

- It stimulates participation
- It encourages diverse ideas & opinions
- It strengthens consensus and buy-in
- It destroys "groupthink" through group synergy
- It's fun (sometimes)
- It fosters leadership maturity in participants

A facilitator who misunderstands or mismanages conflict wastes the group's resources — and his or her credibility.

Recognizing the types Conflict typically happens on two levels: (1) personal or relationship conflicts, and (2) contextual conflicts (cultural, historical, or environmental attitudes and assumptions). The facilitator must be able to recognize these sources of conflicts and how to mitigate them. Tools such as interventions and preventative actions range from subtle to dramatic. Each has its place in the session.

Approaches To Conflict

You have four choices The facilitator will observe participants approach conflict in four basic ways:

- **Competing** — *pursuing own concerns at other's expense.*

- **Accommodating** — *neglecting own concerns to satisfy others.*

- **Avoiding** — *pursuing neither own or other's concerns.*

- **Collaborating** — *pursuing both own and other's concerns mutually and fully.*

The latter attribute, collaboration, is the best approach and the facilitator should reinforce any behaviors supporting it.

- ~~Avoid the issue~~
- ~~Smooth over the issue~~
- ~~Confrontation: WIN-LOSE~~
- **Strive for WIN-WIN solution**

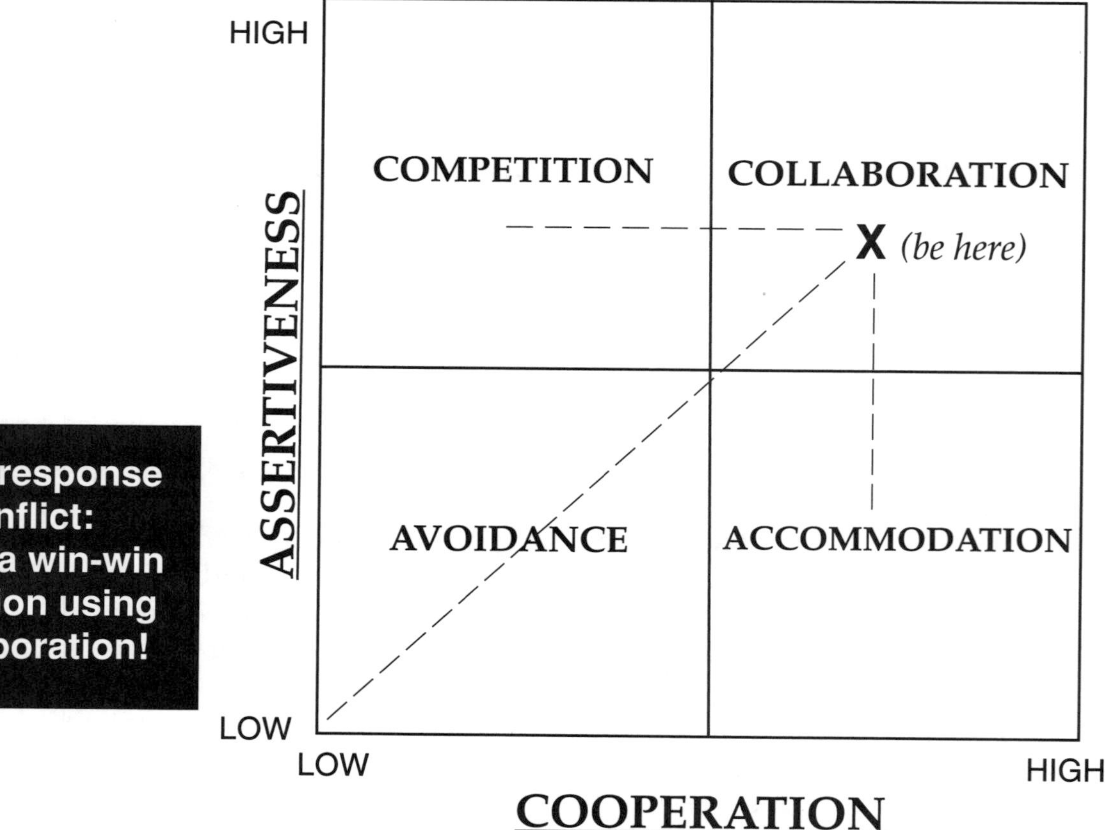

Your response to conflict: seek a win-win solution using collaboration!

Constructive Conflict

It's no good Conflict is destructive when it:

- Diverts energy from more important work
- Creates distrust in the room
- Deepens differences in personal values
- Builds barriers to understanding and cooperation
- Polarizes the room
- Hinders productivity of the session

The best way Behind all conflict are legitimate concerns. Participants hold onto their ideals and expectations because they are important, even self-defining, to each of them. As a result, behind every position is a real, self-driven interest. The facilitator must turn this energy of conflict toward creative purposes. Constructive conflict provides the best way for this because it:

- Stimulates a higher level of understanding
- Enhances constructive communications
- Creates a healthy, positive environment
- Leads to solutions faster

How do you discourage destructive conflict and stimulate constructive conflict? It's simple.

Just do the following:

- **Put things in a larger context**
- **Appeal to higher purpose**
- **Look for win-wins**
- **Reframe disagreements into opportunities**
- **Propose an alternative third way**

REMEMBER: "Meeting space is ego space."

Handling CONFLICT

STEP 1 Clarify objectives

STEP 2 Strive for understanding

STEP 3 Focus on the rationale

STEP 4 Generate alternatives

STEP 5 Allow for "soak time" and take a break

STEP 6 Use humor

Handling DISRUPTIONS

1. Use preventions to avoid the problem
2. Use extinction — ignore the bad behaviors
3. Be a role model for good behaviors
4. Use reinforcement for good behaviors
5. Acknowledge that differences are OK
6. Stimulate involvement & ownership

How do you deal with the disruption caused by a POLARIZED group? Ask the group to (1) stay calm and (2) look at the other side's position. If that doesn't work, then let the group cool-off by either taking a break or adjourning.

Problem Behaviors

- The late comer...
- The early leaver...
- The broken record...
- The Doubting Thomas...
- The headshaker...
- The dropout...
- The whisperer...
- The loudmouth...
- The attacker...
- The interpreter...
- The gossiper...
- The know-it-all...
- The back seat driver...
- The busy body...
- The interrupter...
- The blocker...

Here are some suggestions for the more popular troublemakers. Handling the...

Latecomers Don't confront them before the group. Wait until you can get each person alone and ask why he or she is always late.

Broken Records Use the *Issue Bin* to record this person's comments. Don't address the subject but just record it and move on.

Headshakers Ask the headshaker if he or she has something to share with the group. If that doesn't help then talk to the headshaker during the break. Sometimes the shaker doesn't know that he or she is shaking his or her head!

Loudmouths Walk over and stand next to them. Invade their personal space. Stay there are long as they are boisterous.

Attackers Remind the attacker about the session's groundrule, "No personal attacks."

Keep it PROFESSIONAL and not personal.
Address the BEHAVIOR and not the person.

INTERVENTIONS

IGNORE

PAUSE (be quiet)

PAUSE & LOOK (at the person)

PAUSE & ASK A QUESTION (to the person: "Hey, Bob, what do you think about this?")

WALK OVER TO THE PERSON (and stand nearby)

TOUCH PERSON (lightly... while you continue to talk)

TELL THE GROUP, "LET'S TAKE A BREAK NOW"

TAKE A BREAK & CONFRONT THE PERSON (privately)

CONFRONT THE PERSON DURING THE MEETING

By the Facilitator

Tough Situations

"A competitive world has two possibilities. You can lose. Or, if you want to win, you can change."
— **Lester C. Thurow**

Here are examples behaviors and conditions that can create a tough situation for you...

Behavior	Condition
• Aggressive	• No time
• Passive-Aggressive	• Loud environment
• Passive	• Confidential topic
• Defensive	• Language barrier
	• Physical disability

Remember, no personal attacks! Keep it professional. Period

Watch out for these Tough situations created by unfavorable *conditions* are easier for the facilitator to remedy than tough situations created by *dysfunctional behaviors*. The facilitator can usually eliminate or change adverse conditions in the room or in the possess. It is more common, unfortunately, for the facilitator to be unable to correct undesired behaviors by a participant regardless of numerous interventions. When a participant does not respond to these interventions, we call the resulting dysfunctionality a "difficult behavior."

Difficult behavior = what a person does despite corrective feedback from others.

SECRET: It's OK to let the other person vent. Sometimes that's all they really wanted from the discussion!

Handling Tough Situations

How to handle tough situations

RULE #1 Keep the discussion professional not personal.**

RULE #2 Reschedule the discussion when it gets heated.

**Focus on the success of the business not the person.

Strive for functional behaviors

Passive-Aggressive (PA) This term refers to someone having indirect resistance to authority, responsibility, and obligations. Symptoms include complaining, irritability when faced with demands, and general discontent. Anger is usually expressed indirectly via resistance, delays, losing things, procrastination, and sabotaging one's own efforts or those of others. A PA individual shows habitual, but indirect, resistance to reasonable social and vocational demands. He or she resents authority, and expresses any aggressive impulses passively, for example, by dawdling, feigning ignorance, always showing up late, forgetting, etc. Essentially, PA is a certain maladaptive style of dealing with others.

Dysfunctional Behaviors

- Aggressive
- Passive-Aggressive
- Passive
- Defensive

Functional Behaviors

- Assertive
- Cooperative

Tony Tyrant
Penny Pot-Shot
Arnie Analytical
Wayne Whiner
Eddie Expert
Shirley Staller
Ollie Outtolunch

Preventing Tough Situations

Here's some advice to help the facilitator avoid tough situations

Keep It Professional
Avoid the personal, name-calling, in-your-face, nonproductive behaviors. Keep your focus on the issue and not the person.

Be Unconditionally Constructive
Remember, you're the bigger person here.

Don't Be A Doormat
Remember, you're a human being, too.

Use Active Listening Skills
Never assume you know the mind of the other person so well that you don't have to listen well!

Recognize Differences As Opposed To Difficulties
Difficulties are tough but differences can be good (like diversity). Differences won't impair good communications if you recognize them as such.

Separate "Relationship Issues" from Content Problems
Relationships issues are about how people deal with each other. Segregate how well you work with someone else from the content (topic, problem, etc.) of the discussion. *Say to yourself, "I will treat this person well whether or not I like what he or she thinks or does."*

Beware of Partisan Perceptions
There are two or more sides to every story. Don't contribute to a tough situation by only seeing your side. Remember Steve Covey's famous advice, *"Seek first to understand, then to be understood."*

Balance Reason with Emotion
Keep objectivity and hormones current in the discussion but neither overwhelming the other.

Reschedule the Discussion When It Gets Heated
Give yourself (and the other person) a cooling-off period to regain some objectivity.

Behaviors You'll See in Groups

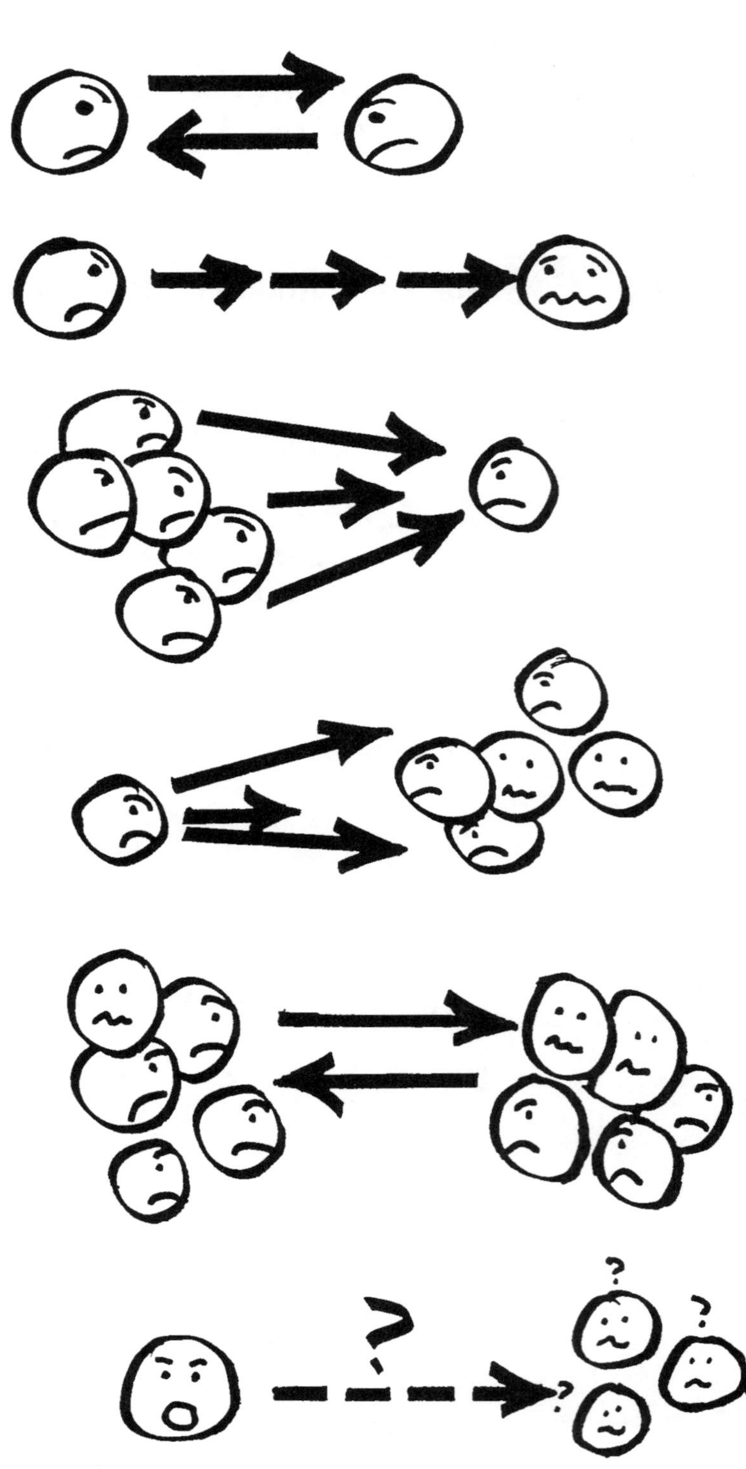

INTERPERSONAL
This behavior is always one-on-one. Both participants are antagonists and openly confront the other during the session. They argue and everyone else just sits there... daydreaming.

ATTACK
This is a one-sided attack. A participant in the room is openly antagonistic towards another (bewildered) individual.

MOB
A group of participants target one person. Watch out — this gets ugly!

LONESOME WARRIOR
Against all odds, this participant is attacking a group in the room. This happy warrior is on a crusade and consumes a great deal of group time.

CHAOS
A very common situation where the room splits into camps. Confusion and lost time are typically the result of these behaviors. This situation commonly ends in a polarized group.

PASSIVE
Having passive participants is the hardest situation for the facilitator to handle. Unlike the previous active conflicts, passive behaviors are very hard to solve because the facilitator cannot determine their causes. Watch out because the passive participant can "erupt" without warning!

Review

- Conflict is expected — eliminate the destructive type and stimulate constructive conflict.

- Key elements for constructive conflict are:
    1. Develop & focus on common goals
    2. No toleration for unresolved conflict
    3. Value differences
    4. Emotions are OK
    5. Understand first
    6. Change is part of the process

- Use preventions and interventions to mitigate destructive conflict.

And remember...

- Use humor appropriately to defuse tension. Reframe the situation in a humorous way but never at the expense of an individual's (or group's) self esteem.

- Physically move people. Make new seating arrangements.

- Turn conflict into positive results by:
    1. Focusing on ideas, not people
    2. Acknowledging everyone's ideas
    3. Keeping it positive using "smoothing" statements
    4. Taking a break so that participants can regain perspective — or cool off.

"He's like a silk handkerchief, all show and no blow."
— **Charles Osgood**

> "Enthusiasm is that kindling spark which marks the difference between the leaders in every activity and the laggards who put in just enough to get by."
>
> — **Johann Friedrich Schiller**

17 GETTING PARTICIPATION

Full potential One of the hardest tasks of being a facilitator is stimulating participation in the group. Always remember that the synergy of a group is what makes facilitation a powerful problem-solving tool. Without everyone's participation, the full potential of the group cannot be realized.

Facilitator behaviors Your job is to create a meeting environment where everyone feels comfortable, even excited, about participating. Whether it is the step of expressing concerns, brainstorming, contributing criteria, or sharing support for actions, your behavior as facilitator determines the level of participation in the room.

It is your skill that ensures participation. This chapter gives you the tools to be a success. Keep your energy focused in three primary areas:

- Create a RISK-FREE environment
- Discourage any put-down phrases and encourage a POSITIVE atmosphere
- Help participants in the room to SPEAK UP.

Benefits for Increase Participation

Why should you devote your time to increasing participation?

Some people might assume that all members of the group are naturally excited about participating in the process. But that's a mistake. Not everyone is the same. Not everyone is enthused about being in the meeting. Some people might be preoccupied with other issues. Animosity might exist between people.

As the facilitator, you cannot possibly know everything that is influencing participants' behaviors. But you can diligently take steps to minimize them and at the same time enhance participation.

But why?

Participant involvement increases the productivity and effectiveness of the team. It allows for streamlining and innovation of work methods and procedures. Participation also finds new ways of flexible deployment for action items.

Increased participation fundamentally supports the concept of quality improvement since it draws on the input of all team members. Furthermore, it builds commitment in group members. Having a high level of group participation also reinforces the desired behaviors of cooperation and coordination within a team.

GROUP SYNERGY

The total contribution of the group becomes greater than the independent contributions of its individuals.

Besides these benefits, the leader will witness a higher level of customer satisfaction, both internal customers and external customers, as a byproduct of increased group participation. Less direct supervision will be required afterwards because of greater involvement and buy-in of the group members. Greater synergism will yield better ideas, better commitment, and better support by those affected by the group's output.

Ways To Promote Participation

- Make eye-contact with the person
- Ask questions that are "open-ended"
- Use silence — wait for answers
- Make comments reinforcing participants and cause members to acknowledge each other
- Call directly on a person
- Post key ideas or statements on the wall
- Create the expectation that members come prepared
- Avoid interventions that are "win-lose" and seek "win-win" ones
- Share with the group your participation expectations of them
- Lighten up and use humor
- Be positive and non-judgemental
- Give your attention to the speaker
- Use proper body language
- Share personal examples

Facilitator's Skill = Better Participation

Create a RISK-FREE environment

- Use positive and encouraging remarks.
- Show an "open-minded" attitude by not criticizing ideas or comments.
- Use positive nonverbal communication (body language, voice tone, etc.).

Encourage a POSITIVE ATMOSPHERE

Avoid "put-down" statements like:
- *"It won't work"*
- *"We already tried that!"*
- *"It's not in the budget"*

Instead, say things like:
- *"OK - let's write that down!"*
- *"Thank you!"*
- *"That's helpful... any more comments or ideas?"*

Help participants to SPEAK UP

- Probe for additional information (see "5 Whys" later in this chapter).
- Ask open-ended questions (i.e. those requiring more than "yes" or "no").
- Tactfully manage overly-vocal people who dominate the conversations.
- Call on quiet people — try asking for their thoughts or "expert" opinions.

KEEP THE PROCESS MOVING...

Here's a simple tool to keep things moving and group participation high. If you hit a snag, just ask the group, "Are we altogether? Can me move along?" Have them respond using one of the three thumb signals shown here.

"I agree"

"I don't know - let's talk more"

If someone gives a "thumbs down" signal, they are required to provide the group with two things (see box below).

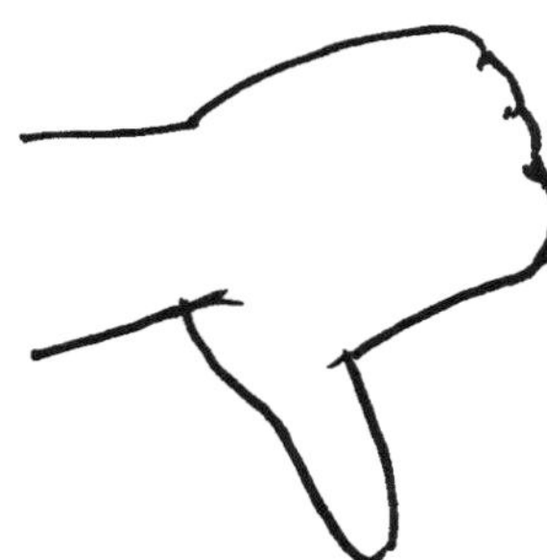

"No - I can't support it** "

Can be also as a CONSENSUS tool

** If someone indicates a thumbs-down "No - I can't support it" then he or she MUST provide the group with two things:

(1) He or she must EXPLAIN WHY (and the justification "I don't like it" is NOT acceptable here), and
(2) He or she must present the group with ANOTHER SOLUTION as an alternative.

NOTE: *It is your job as facilitator to make this process step clear to the group.*

Increase Participation by...
PROVIDING THINGS THAT MOTIVATE

Different things motivate people. As a facilitator, you might want to find out what motivates some participants in the group. Here are seven areas to look at:

1. The need for **achievement**
2. The need for **power**
3. The need for **affiliation**
4. The need for **autonomy**
5. The need for **esteem**
6. The need for **safety** and **security**
7. The need for **equity**

You will pick up hints if you pay close attention to participants' behaviors. For someone not participating in the process, try fulfilling one or more of the needs lacking for that person. Try it.

Increase Participation by...
CREATING AN INCLUSIVE ENVIRONMENT

Creating an atmosphere where everyone feels included is very important to building trust and increasing participation. Here are four rules to follow to help foster that inclusive environment.

- Focus on **issues** - not personalities
- Focus on **interests** - not positions
- Create **options** to satisfy mutual and separate interests
- Evaluate options with **standards** — not with power

KEEP THE PROCESS MOVING...

Do you need clear explanations from group participants? Try using the "Five Whys" technique shown below. Be courteous - but persistent in asking "why?" until you get a complete answer. Try it!

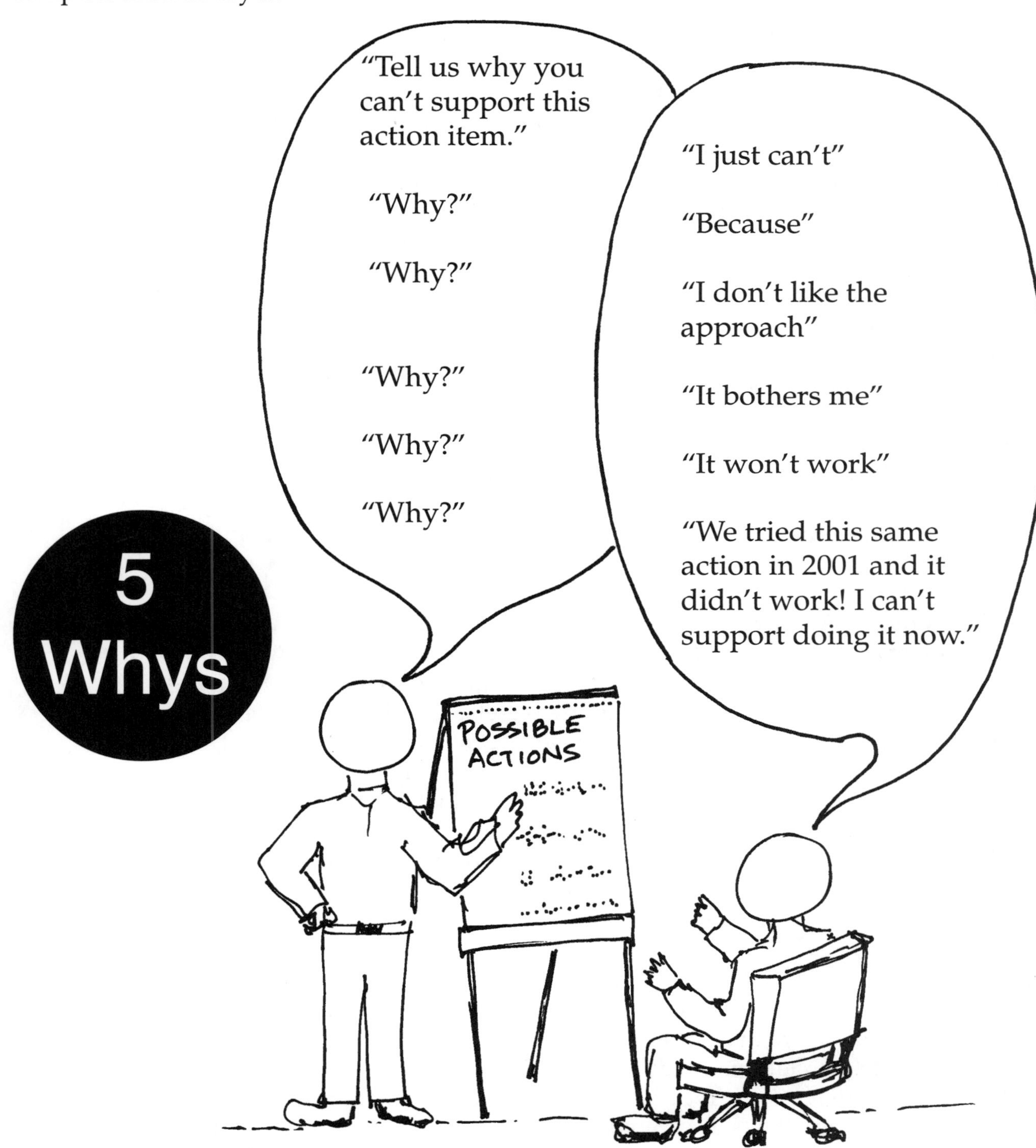

Outside Facilitator's Control

It's not always your fault A facilitator must understand that he or she cannot always solve the problem of poor participation. Sometimes there are events or conditions beyond the control of the facilitator. Sometimes the culture of the organization has created such an adverse environment that even participants with the best intentions cannot raise the energy to participate.

Lack of participation The facilitator depends on the participation of group members to make the collaborative problem-solving process work well. In some sessions, group members are energized and the process moves quickly. At other times, however, the facilitator may experience subtle or open resistance. People are quiet, they refuse to contribute ideas, or just don't show up for the session. Despite every facilitation "trick" used to stimulate participation, it appears that no one is interested in working the process.

Feeling involved People wonder why group members act like this. It is especially perplexing to management personnel. From their viewpoint, everyone should be excited to participate in problem solving teams because it is a wonderful opportunity to help the organization. When lackluster participation occurs, management often feels bewildered and annoyed — especially since they have freed participants from their normal work duties and bestowed upon the participants the "honor" of being involved. But the solution can only be found by looking at it from the participants' point of view, not management's viewpoint. It's all about being treated fairly in the organization.

Perceived equity Are the participants "bad" people? No. Are they lazy? Not necessarily. Participants behave is such low-energy or resistant ways for many reasons. They may be worried about personal problems. They could be concerned with job security and financial threats. Or the participants could feel cheated or mistreated in their jobs — and choose not help the organization solve its problems. This revenge can manifest itself as subtle resistance to participating in a problem-solving process. Examples would be passive-aggressive behaviors like withholding information, creating roadblocks, or acting indifferently. When acting like this, participants are trying to deliver "payback" for past harm done to them — they are trying to gain some degree of personal equity. Simply, they could be trying to establish their own perceived equity as a human being in the organization.

The facilitator's solution When the facilitator senses this resistance the best course of action is to call a time-out. Tell the group, "I sense a reluctance to participate by the group. Can anyone share their feelings about this?" Go off-the-record (no recording on flipcharts) and talk about this situation. Do NOT accuse or judge the participants but just listen. Sometimes this "gripe session" is enough therapy to resolve the perceived equity problem. If not, the facilitator should end the session and discuss the situation with the leader.

Review

Getting Participation

- Create a risk-free environment
- Encourage a positive atmosphere
- Help participants to speak up
- Keep the process moving — use hand signals to get group input
- Create an inclusive environment

And remember...

• Motivating participants to participate is not difficult once they see the personal benefits of being involved. The facilitator should take every opportunity to play their favorite radio station, WII-FM (“What’s In It For Me).

• The resistance arising from the lack of participants’ perceived equity in the organization happens occasionally. If the facilitator senses this reluctance to participate, then he or she should discuss it informally with the group.

"The leader must have infectious optimism."
— **Field General Bernard Montgomery**

> "To be trusted is a greater compliment than to be loved."
>
> — **Robert W. Service**

18 BUILDING TRUST

Why so important? Trust is the cornerstone of a successful facilitation session. Without it, participants find it difficult to accept interventions by the facilitator. Without it, a facilitator must substitute control for influence. Without it, having a neutral, collaborative problem solving process is suspect. The facilitator must work to maintain the trust of the participants.

Bigger impact "Doing what you say you'll do" is the best description of trust. Its importance cascades through an organization and affects every employee. Having trust in a collaborative problem-solving session is critical to its success. The following headlines show the paradigms most employees have about trust:

"Lack of management trust is the biggest barrier to building high involvement organizations." — Development Dimensions International survey

"61% don't believe management tells them the truth." — Council for Communications Management Study

"Only 38% trust employers to keep their promises." — Princeton Survey Research Associates

"TRUST BUSTERS"

What to know what kills trust in a session? Here's a list of actual comments made by participants compiled over several years of collaborative problem-solving sessions.

- "Opinions of participants are not valued by the facilitator."
- "Lack of consistency in how the facilitator treats the participants."
- "Theft of ideas permitted during session."
- "Participants talking behind others' backs."
- "Failure to resolve issue — no closure."
- "Leader is permitted to dictate the group's decisions."
- "Facilitator is not honest."
- "Participants are not honest."
- "Facilitator is not accountable to the group."
- "Facilitator does not follow the process."

- "Facilitator does not enforce ground rules in the room."
- "Interference by leader, management, or home office is allowed."
- "Constant confusion exists within the group."
- "Participants don't treat each other well."
- "Poor communication of 'what's going on' by facilitator or leader."
- "Facilitator allows participants to put personal agenda over the process."
- "Facilitator does not draw out specifics and allows unsubstantiated generalizations."
- "Facilitator is emotional and reactive in guiding the process — instead of proactive and rational."

WOW! This is a good list of what NOT to do!

Attributes For Having Trust

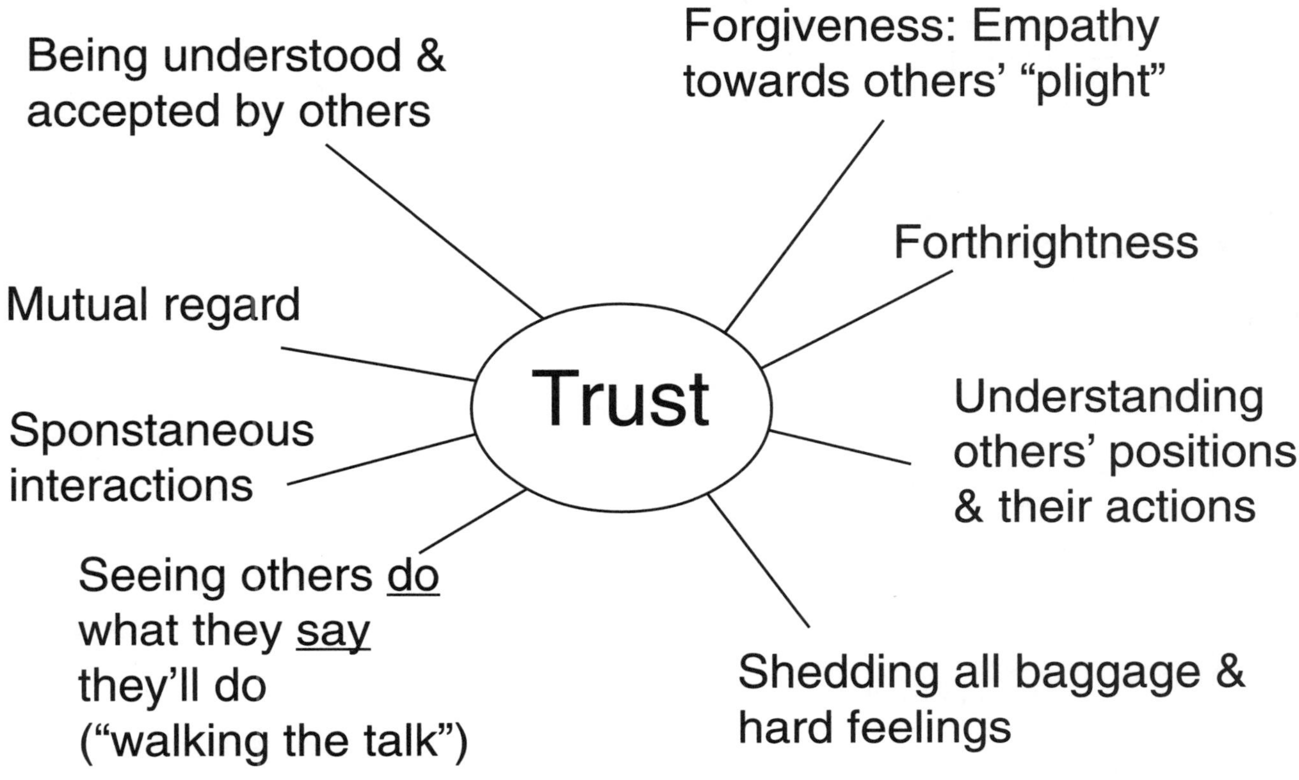

> "Trust is like money — it's tough to get and easy to lose."
> — **Sid**

What you'll see in groups lacking trust...

- Comments like "I don't care" or "I'll take care of myself"
- No respect for each other
- Open or subtle hostility
- Abruptness — such as interrupting or cutting others off while talking
- Behaviors reflecting low self-confidence
- Withholding information
- Defensive body language (crossed arms, holding self, sitting apart from others)

Key Elements of Trust

Planned action The facilitator must be proactive in building trust with the group. Do not assume that "things will take care of themselves" and trust will flourish within the room. The facilitator must undertake planned, discrete actions to behave in a manner that builds trust. In the box below is a list of elements and attributes that can help you build a trusting relationship within the room.

> Practicing good communications

> Being consistent in your behaviors

> Building positive experiences & history

> Respecting individuals

> Acting honestly

> Showing integrity

> Being sincere in your relationships

> Striving for common understanding

> Being accountable

> Showing conviction in your beliefs

> Forgiving others for mistakes and behaviors

> Showing sincere courtesy

> Acting with selflessness

> Showing genuine concern for relationships

Facilitator's Trust-Builders

Here are specific actions that the facilitator should do to gain the trust of participants.

1. Respect each member of the group.

2. Be a role model of trust: "Do exactly what you say you'll do."

3. Put the (realistic) needs of the group ahead of yours.

4. Show empathy for the group.

5. Be open & honest.

6. Listen — listen — listen!

7. Sincerely value the group's desires.

RESPECT THE DIGNITY,
THE WORTH,
AND THE CREATIVE POTENTIAL
OF EVERY HUMAN BEING
IN THE ORGANIZATION

Specific Actions For Building Trust

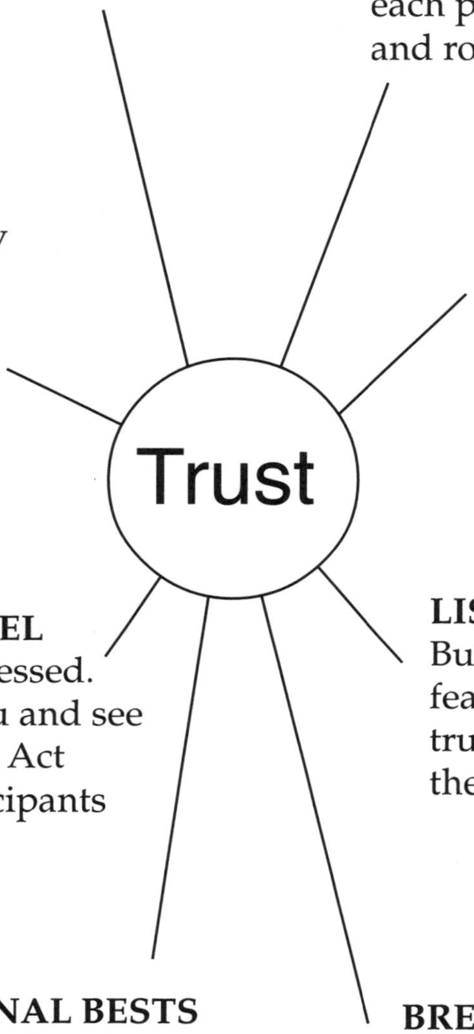

COMMUNICATE WITH THE GROUP "What's Going On."
Hold regular updates from participants on news and activities - both at work and at home.

SHARE BACKGROUNDS
Go around the room and have each participants share their job and role in the group.

STYLE INVENTORY
Have the participants do a survey/inventory of their personal style. Discuss the different styles and their needs.

SAFETY NETS
Build a list of participants' ideas of what would create a safe and trusting environment in the room. Post it on the wall.

Trust

YOU AS ROLE MODEL
This cannot be overstressed. Participants watch you and see more than you realize. Act trustworthy and participants will do the same.

LIST OF LAND MINES
Build a list of participants' fears and problems that inhibit trust and progress. Post it on the wall.

BREAKOUT: PERSONAL BESTS
Break the participants into small groups and have each person share past successes with similar collaborative teams.

BREAKS = PRIORITY
Breaks are one of the best tools for relationship building. Plan them and make sure they happen!

Review

- Be a role model for trustworthiness

- Building trust takes planned, specific action by the facilitator

- Watch your body language — it signals distrust or uncaring

- Listen and watch for participants' comments and behaviors that signal "no trust"

- Avoid half-truths and "half-information" — full disclosure is a must!

- The facilitator's behavior outside the session can also destroy trust because "word always gets back" to the group about your outside comments and actions.

And remember...

- Show that you care. Here four actions for facilitators to use:
    1. Listen to the participants
    2. Don't allow anyone to abuse anyone else
    3. Don't let the group or any participant pay for your mistakes
    4. Help out during tough times — be there and help!

> "Most people would be trusted more and respected more if they said less and did more."
>
> — **Dr. Aubrey Daniels**

> Misery loves (your) company.
> — **Gail Snyder**

19 MANAGING YOUR STRESS

Stress is one of the leading causes of disease in the United States.

Always stressful It's not all fame and glory as a facilitator. Having the responsibility to guide a group of people through a long number of process steps is not always pleasant. There is no doubt that being a facilitator is a stressful job. You cannot escape it — but you can take steps to mitigate it.

Doing the steps Fortunately, stress is part of everyday life. It drives a facilitator to move the process ahead. In fact, stress makes facilitators perform better because it creates an anxiety to succeed. However, when it becomes excessive, stress can be counterproductive and facilitators lose their ability to remain enthusiastic and flexible in managing the process — and the group. Recognition is the first step in managing the stress of being a facilitator. The second step is knowing how to lessen the impact of the stress. And the third step is knowing how to avoid situations creating the stress.

Recognizing Stress

What is stress? Stress is the response of the body and mind to a situation or event. Things causing stress are referred to as *stressors*. Life is filled with stressors, both large and small, that are unavoidable. Driving, shopping, preparing reports, and paying monthly bills are very common stressors in our society. The trouble starts when the number of stressors and their importance become so large that people cannot cope with them. In the case of facilitation, stressors arise from various duties such as handling pre-meeting arrangements, working process steps, handling questions, or challenging the group to move ahead. Sorry, but these stressors cannot be avoided. The trick to helping you is minimizing their number.

Rethinking stress Listed below are popular stressors in facilitation sessions:

- uncooperative participants
- poorly-behaved participants
- strategic dilemma (strategic moments)
- fear of misspelling words while recording
- enforcing the process rules

Stress indicators Facilitators must be able to recognize the effects of stress in themselves — and in participants. Listed below are useful stress indicators:

- headaches
- emotional outbursts
- rapid heart rate
- upset stomach
- sweaty/trembling hands
- weak feeling
- always tired, low energy
- overeating
- loss of appetite
- muscle tension (neck & shoulders)
- increased smoking
- restlessness
- can't concentrate
- irritable - can't get along with others
- depressed
- blaming others

Tips For Handling Stress

Get enough rest

Eat a good breakfast

Laugh more

Exercise 30 minutes each day

1 Practice deep breathing

Exhale as far as you can and then slowly fill your lungs

2 Close your eyes, relax and visualize

Picture yourself in a pleasant situation. Relax. Breathe deeply. You're OK!

3 Take a break

Say, "Let's take a fifteen minute break" during the session.

4 Ask yourself, "How important is it?"

For those situations causing you stress, ask this question to yourself, "What's the worst that could happen? What are the chances it will?"

5 Act on the problem

Don't delay addressing the problem. Confront it — now!

Reduce or eliminate caffeine, alcohol, cigarettes

Don't sweat the small stuff

Delegate

Do unpleasant tasks first

Take six deep breaths - slowly

Want more information about danger signals? Turn the page!

Danger Signs

Burnout

The facilitator (or the participant) becomes unable to cope. All desire to work and the ability to focus are gone. There are no worries anymore since the person is nearly catatonic.

Brownout

The facilitator (or the participant) "tunes-out" from things happening because of an immense preoccupation with worry. The individual cannot remember conversations. The individual cannot remember where he or she left items. The person asks the same question several times, unaware of repeating himself. These behaviors create frustration, and sometimes anger, in everyone associated with the person. Stress brownouts are not a burnout — yet — but these behaviors are important warning signs.

Communications Misfires

Communication misfires typically occur when there is a mismatch in expectations between people. This could happen during a facilitation session when the facilitator mistakenly (but sincerely) believes the group is excited and enthusiastic about one of the steps — say, brainstorming possibilities. But when they don't behave with the expected enthusiastic behaviors, the facilitator can become perplexed, even angry, at the group's apathy. This mismatch between facilitator's expectation and group behavior creates anxiety, anger and stress — both in the facilitator and in the group.

Avoiding Stress In The Long Run

Don't beat your head against the wall! Be kind to yourself!

1. Exercise regularly.

2. Learn relaxation techniques (biofeedback, meditation, deep breathing).

3. Get a hobby.

4. Find a place to escape to — inside your home or office, or outside (woods, mountains, creekside, park, seashore, field, quiet room).

5. Schedule time in your day for relaxation and fun. Do it!

6. Reduce or eliminate tobacco, caffeine, alcohol, sugar, salt, carbonated beverages, or similar substances from your diet.

7. Eliminate the sources of stress in your life. Think about it — you'll recognize them.

8. Be kind to yourself. Life isn't a movie and you're not perfect! Don't be so hard on yourself! Be nice to yourself!

Preparation beforehand *always* reduces your stress during the session!

Learn To Say "NO"

Say no quickly Reduce your stress by saying "no" before the agony of indecision sets in. Don't agonize when facilitating — say "no" quickly!

Say no politely Reduce your stress by remaining pleasant and not escalating the stress of the situation. When you facilitate, say "no" with tack and politeness.

Say no with an alternative Reduce your stress by offering an alternate solution or method. Someone might prematurely ask, "Let's go to lunch now" and you could respond, "No. We'll finish our brainstorming first and then we'll break for lunch."

Reduce your stress Remember that the facilitator owns the process and has the privilege to say "no" when facilitating. Doing it quickly, politely, and, if needed, with an alternative. Being proactive will reduce your stress. Try it!

Don't procrastinate! Learn to say "no"!

Review

- Learn to say "no"
- Stop — and take 6 deep breaths
- The best cure for stress = identify its cause
- Time management is a good stress reducer
- Set limits — or else delegate more
- Have a good laugh — often!

And remember...

- **Your prescription for reducing stress:** Do something about it!

- **Watch for signs of burnout** — in yourself and in participants.

"Meetings are indispensable when you don't want to do anything."
— **J.K. Galbraith**, *Ambassador's Journal*, 1969

V

Appendices

20. Do's & Don'ts
21. Frequently-Asked Questions
22. Selected Resources
23. Examples You Can Use
24. Index

"When you come to a fork in the road, take it."

— **Yogi Berra**

> "If A equals success, then the formula is A equals X plus Y plus Z. X is work. Y is play. Z is keep your mouth shut."
> — **Albert Einstein**

20 DO'S & DON'TS

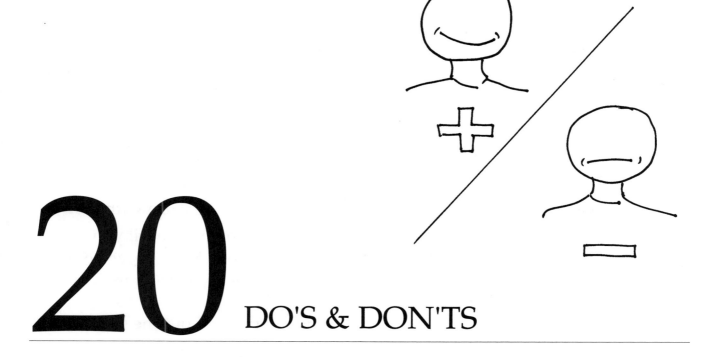

Now that you have had an opportunity to learn the process steps of being a facilitator, it's time to learn some lessons from experienced facilitators.

New or inexperienced facilitators may be discouraged when a group doesn't participate or show any enthusiasm for the process. That's natural and happens often. Just remember that people act differently in groups than individually... and don't be discouraged.

Each facilitation session is unique. There are, however, a number of rules that help you avoid catastrophe. Following these do's and don'ts will help you succeed as a neutral facilitator.

I guarantee it.

Don't

- Don't argue
- Don't get angry
- Don't threaten the group
- Don't tolerate personal attacks upon anyone
- Don't let the group discussion get too far off the subject
- Don't write on flipcharts with a yellow-colored pen
- Don't be afraid to ask "What would the group like to do with that?"
- Don't forget that you are NEUTRAL... and remain so until you tell the group that you are "taking off your facilitator's hat" to give your personal opinion on the subject... otherwise, keep your opinions to yourself!
- Don't let a session run longer than two hours without the group's permission
- Don't be late

Do

- **Meet with the leader** before the group-facilitation session
- Be **early** to the group session
- Have the **room set up** and **flipcharts prepared** beforehand
- Have a **plan** for the process steps you will follow
- Have a **backup plan** if you get stuck in the process
- **Listen** to the needs & wants of the group
- Be **flexible** with the group
- Be **firm**
- Use **humor**
- Be **positive** & upbeat
- **End on-time** each group-facilitation session

Helpful Hints

• When you're in front of the group as the facilitator, it's OK to **be entertaining** because, as they say in show business, "entertainment is the spice of life!" And people love to be entertained! Hemorrhoidal behavior is *not* a desirable trait for any facilitator.

• Use lots of **colors** in diagrams & drawings. Why? Because people like color!

• Keep things **moving quickly**... forge ahead and keep going. If you don't, people will get bored and disengage themselves from the process.

• Always be **one step ahead** of the group (example: have the next flipchart sheet ready to use for the next topic or process step).

• Always **listen**. And if you cannot, don't try to fake it! Instead, say "I'm sorry, but I didn't catch what you just said..."

• Keep **focused** on your objective as a facilitator. You are there to **get a job done**. You are not being paid by the flipchart page completed... so help the group overcome wasteful tangents, arguments, or roadblocks... and keep moving!

• Don't be scared to occasionally **"let out the leash"** when the group's discussion ventures into new territory... it may pay dividends with new ideas or the a better understanding of the topic by some members.

• If you get stuck and don't know what to say, then just tell the group, **"Let's take a break!"**

• Schedule meetings for **two hours** in length. Groups are just getting "warmed up" at one hour and start to get tired after two hours.

• Be positive!

DO THIS

	SITUATION	YOU DO THIS...
	Two people in the group are talking to each other (a "sidebar") and have become a distraction to others.	*Stopping talking. Let your silence grab their attention.*
	The leader starts to monopolize the meeting - talking continually! You start to sense that members of the group are now reluctant to speak up.	*Break in and say, "What do other people think about this?" Make eye contact with anyone else BUT the leader when asking this question.*
	Some people in the group has a confused look on their face when you say, "OK. Let's start to list some possible criteria for solving our issue."	*Pay attention to the eyes. Stop and ask the group, "Does anyone need help understanding WHERE we are in the process? Or what criteria are?"*
	Someone in the group suddenly gathers her things and walks out of the meeting. She says nothing... just leaves!	*Just keep going. Don't disrupt the flow of the session. You can find out why during the break.*
	During the brainstorming of possibilities, someone raises his hand and says, "We've tried that before several times and it has NEVER worked! Why should we waste our time now?"	*Refer the person to the group's rule: "No criticism of ideas."*
	Someone walks in late... fifteen minutes after the meeting's start.	*My motto is "Start on time and NO rewind." Don't reinforce the latecomer's tardiness by stopping to explain what's gone on. Even if the tardy person is the leader. Sorry... it's not fair to everyone else who arrived on time!*

DO remember that facilitation sessions experience the same cycle of development as teams.

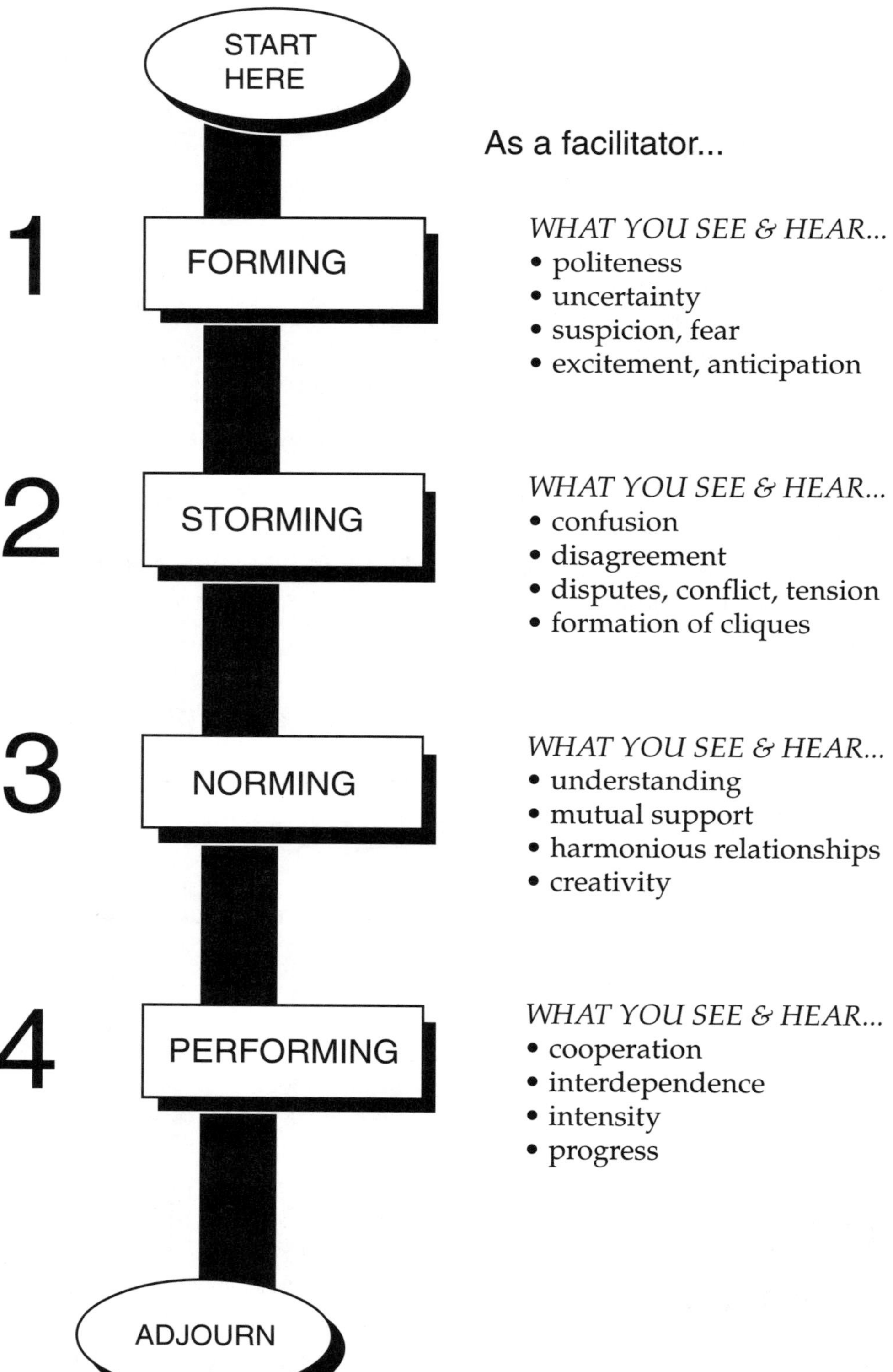

As a facilitator...

WHAT YOU SEE & HEAR...
- politeness
- uncertainty
- suspicion, fear
- excitement, anticipation

WHAT YOU SEE & HEAR...
- confusion
- disagreement
- disputes, conflict, tension
- formation of cliques

WHAT YOU SEE & HEAR...
- understanding
- mutual support
- harmonious relationships
- creativity

WHAT YOU SEE & HEAR...
- cooperation
- interdependence
- intensity
- progress

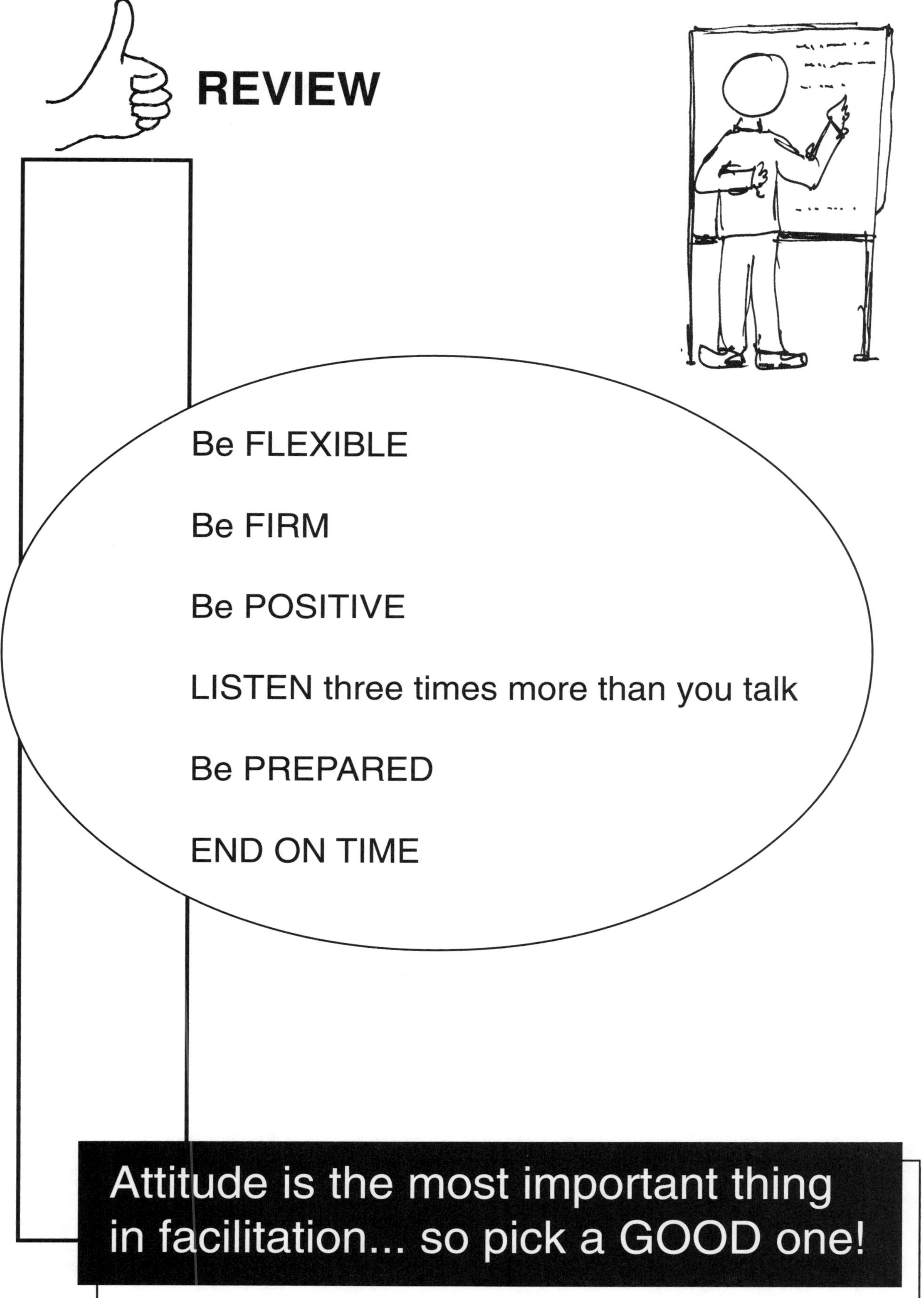
REVIEW
Be FLEXIBLE
Be FIRM
Be POSITIVE
LISTEN three times more than you talk
Be PREPARED
END ON TIME
Attitude is the most important thing in facilitation... so pick a GOOD one!

"It took me a lifetime to become an overnight success."
— **Dr. J**

> "Experience enables you to recognize a mistake when you make it again."
>
> — **Franklin P. Jones**

21 FREQUENTLY-ASKED QUESTIONS

Here are answers to questions frequently asked about facilitation:

Question #1
"I've been asked to facilitate a group next week. The group is not my work group but they work in the same building. I've never done this before. What should I do to get started?"

Answer
Your first task is to study the process steps in facilitation (issue, concerns, possibilities, criteria, action, check) in Part II, "Steps For Successful Facilitation."

The second step is to meet with the group's leader before the facilitation session. Cover the checklist in Chapter 11, "You And The Leader."

The third step is the pre-meeting logistics: arrange the first meeting, reserve the room, notify the meeting participants, prepare your flipcharts & visual aids. See the balance of Part III, "Doing It!" for detailed information.

Question #2
"My boss says that she will facilitate an upcoming meeting with our work group. I'm concerned about her remaining an effective facilitator. What do you think?"

Answer
Your concern is a valid one.

It is very, very hard to be a group leader and a neutral facilitator at the same time. Despite her best effort and sincere actions to remain neutral, the group might have some lingering suspicion that she has a hidden agenda.

It is best to find someone outside the group who has no interest in the outcome. That way, the group is more likely to open up and express its true feelings... and the leader can relax and participate in the process without the pressure of managing the process. Remember, the prime objectives are building trust in the process and maximizing group participation. If your boss cannot accomplish these objectives, then find someone who can!

Question #3
"I write like a third grader. If I have to record group comments and ideas on a flipcharts, then I'll be so nervous that I won't be able to manage the process! What should I do?"

Answer
Simple. Recruit someone who has good handwriting to help you.

Appoint a scribe

Having a scribe assist the facilitator is not unusual. In fact, it frees the facilitator to focus more on what is being said by the participants. Plus, it expands group involvement. If you cannot persuade someone to do it for the entire meeting, then split the writing responsibilities among several people in the group.

You will be pleasantly surprised how many people will gladly assist you in this area!

Question #4

"My work group has had several experiences where their recommendations have been shot down by people outside the group after a series of facilitated meetings. It's almost hopeless now. Nobody wants to spend the time creating action items because someone is always ready to pounce on us afterwards. Any suggestions?"

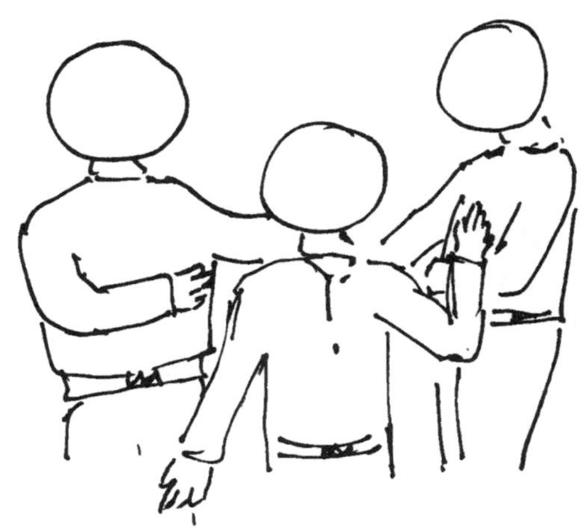

Answer

This is very common. People that ambush your ideas and actions are known as "duck hunters" or "reed people" because, like hunters, they typically wait in the reeds, pop up, and start "blasting away" at your ideas.

The trick to success is to include these people in your decision-making process.

By virtue of their desire to shoot down your ideas, they must be stakeholders in the output of your group. It is very important to identify these people at your first meeting. The questions to ask the group are, "Who else should be involved in this process? Who out there has some vested interest in what this group decides? Who is going to give us any damaging flak over our actions?"

Question #5

"I've volunteered to facilitate a meeting with my group. Before I send out the meeting announcement, shouldn't I tell them how long the session will last?"

2 hours is the perfect length

Answer

Good idea. Experience has taught me two things about groups and meeting length: (1) at one hour, a group is just getting warmed-up and participation starts to "take off," and (2) at two hours, a group is typically tired and their energy level is low.

Recommendation? *Schedule the meeting to end after two hours.* If, after two hours, they want to continue then keep going! Just ask every thirty minutes thereafter if they want to continue... it's up to them.

Question #6
"During last week's meeting that I facilitated, the group kept asking me for my ideas of what they should do. They wanted my suggestions for solutions to the problem. What should I say?"

Answer
Remember, you are a *neutral* facilitator! You control the process and the group owns the content.

Remain neutral

When a group asks you for input on a solution, they're asking you to be involved in the content. If you want to remain neutral you cannot get involved. It's tempting... but don't do it! *Resist the urge to be brilliant!*

What should you do? First, remind the group that you are a neutral facilitator and cannot answer content-oriented questions. Second, "reflect" the question back to the group by asking them, "What do *others* in the group think...?"

If you feel very, very strongly about giving some input and are willing to risk your neutral position, see Question #7 below.

Question #7
"I feel very strongly about the issue being worked by the group. I want to stay a neutral facilitator but I feel that I must speak out! What should I do?"

Answer
OK, this situation occurs to every facilitator.

You may be a expert on the issue. You may have intimate knowledge of the subject. Or you might have some new data about the topic. In any case, you have a burning feeling deep inside you that says, "Tell the group!" *And you sincerely believe that what you will say about the content will help the group solve its problem.*

Here's what you do. First, say, "I'm going to take off my neutral facilitator's hat for a minute." Second, walk from the front of the group to the rear of the room and say what you must. Finally, when finished, return to the front of the group and say, "I'm now putting my neutral facilitator's hat back on." *Warning: Do not over do this! It's acceptable to do this once or twice a meeting at the most!*

Question #8
"Do I have to prepare my flipcharts before the meeting? Why can't I just make them as I go? "

Answer
If it's an informal, spur-of-the-moment problem solving meeting, you can.

But, if it's a future meeting, informal or not, it's always best to prepare the flipcharts ahead of time. Why? Three reasons:

First, it saves you the embarrassment of forgetting the next step. *With prepared flipcharts, simply flip the page over and there's the next step!* (Hey, with all the discussion and talk, it's easy to forget what you're doing next!)

Second, the pause and quiet in the room while you prepare the blank flipchart is an interruption to the process flow. It creates opportunities for off-track discussions while you are writing. *If your flipcharts are prepared then you can move along from step to step without hesitation!*

Third, you will create the illusion of an expert facilitator who cares by being prepared! A group will *also* think, "Hey! If she takes the time to prepare those flipcharts, then this activity must be important... and we must be important, too!"

Question #9
"When I facilitate my group, there are always side conversations going on in the room. It's distracting to the process! How do I stop people from talking on the side like this? "

Your silence creates attention

Answer
First Step: When you hear the sidebar discussion... stop talking. Your silence will be noticed and the sidebar should end.

Step Two: If the first step does not work, then you should continue talking while slowly walk over to the individuals who are talking and stand near them. Your physical presence will be a strong indicator to them that you notice their poor behavior.

Step Three: If the first two steps do not work, then call a "time-out" and ask the group, "Don't we have a rule that says '*One person talks at a time*'?" This will really get their attention!

Question #10
"I'm going to start facilitating a new group next week. I met with the group's leader yesterday. How do I know the leader will *behave* herself during our meetings?"

Answer
Surely you discussed this with the leader during your initial meeting! But sometimes leaders have a short memory and revert back to her or his old behaviors of "command and control" during a meeting.

ACTIVELY involve others

You as the facilitator must protect the rights of all participants in the meeting. If the leader starts to take control, try these interventions:

Intervention #1: After the leader makes a decisive remark, ask the group, "What do others in the group think...?"

Intervention #2: If the leader continues to dominate the process, just announce, "Let's take a break!" Then talk to the leader and remind the leader of your role as facilitator (NOT her or his role as leader) to guide the process.

Question #11
"Yikes! Yesterday I got stuck and froze-up while facilitating. I couldn't think what to do next! What should I do if I cannot figure out what the next step is while in front of the group?"

Answer
Your best move would be to announce, "Let's take a break!"

During the break you will have time to regain your composure and think about your next step. You will also have time to refer to your reference material (like this text) or talk to knowledgeable people in the group about what to do.

If you cannot determine a next step during this break, then secure an *overnight recess* by suggesting to the group, "Can we quit for today and meet again tomorrow?" This will give you enough time to call me for advice.

Question #12
"Getting a group to consensus is so hard! Why can't we just vote to make a decision? It would be much faster!"

Answer
Sure, voting is always faster. But voting causes more damage to individuals in a group than the value of the time saved. Consider the following three points against voting:

Don't vote

First, voting forces most people to establish a position that is very, very hard to change *without looking foolish.*

Second, voting can heavily influences by *peer pressure.* Look at how people raise their hands only after looking around the room to see who's hands are up. That behavior cannot reflect true conviction about a decision!

Third, voting that uses a majority to decide the outcome *ignores the needs of the minority.* In other words, those individuals that "lose" in a vote... do you expect them to immediately abandon their convictions? In most instances, the minority looks for revenge.

Nonbinding "straw votes" are fine as indicators of where people are... but make it clear that the vote is just that, nonbinding. *The best thing you can do is to talk, talk, talk until everyone feels comfortable with supporting the group's decision.*

Question #13
"There's one team member is very rude and antagonistic towards others in our group meeting. It is starting to affect attendance at our meetings. What should I do?"

Answer
You as the facilitator own the process. It is appropriate for you to take action in this situation to mitigate the threatening environment created by this person.

My recommendation is to extinguish this problem behavior immediately. A first step would be to ask the person, "Bob, I sense that you are very angry about something and I also feel that it is hurting our process. Can you help me understand your feelings?"

Warning: Don't start a debate in front of the group with this person. If the problem behavior does not stop, then call a time out and talk to the person privately. Tell him or her that their behavior is counterproductive to the process. *It is appropriate for you to ask him or her to leave the meeting.*

> "I have found that I make few mistakes in life when I believe the best about people."
>
> — **Dr. Robert Schuller**

> "All of us are smarter than any of us."
> — **D. & R. Johnson**

22 SELECTED RESOURCES

This book is an excellent source of information and examples but no single source is sufficient to become a good facilitator. Now that you have read this book, it is time for you to get more training in collaborative problem-solving skills.

Printed material There are many excellent books on facilitation, group dynamics, consensus-building, and the processes surrounding collaborative decision-making. A selected list is provided in this chapter for the reader's use. Search engines in online book sellers' websites are the easiest way to locate additional books.

Classroom training As a step beyond reading about it, there is one company that teaches it and does an excellent job. Interaction Associates, Inc. *does* professional facilitation and also teaches classes at its San Francisco office. More information is provided in this chapter.

Experience makes you better There is no substitute for experience. My personal experience shows that the best way to become a good facilitator is to **do it**. There is no substitute for actually getting up in front of a group and being a facilitator! Do it!

Printed Text

I've compiled a list of useful books to help you be a better facilitator. The list is divided into four areas: meeting skills, people skills, flipchart & visual tools, and facilitation skills. Each book is very helpful and worth your time to read.

Meeting Skills

How to Make Meetings Work!, Michael Doyle & David Straus. Berkley Books, 1976. ISBN 0-425-13870-4. *Topics: What goes wrong at meetings, win/win solutions, being a good facilitator, planning your meeting, making meeting rooms work, tools for solving problems in groups, training yourself.*

Effective Meeting Skills. Marion E. Haynes. Crisp Publications, Inc., 1988. ISBN 0-931961-33-5. *Topics: planning meetings, leader's role, generating alternatives, handling difficult situations, how to improve meetings, a model for effective meetings.*

Meetings That Work, Marlene Caroselli. SkillPath Publications, Inc., 1992. ISBN 1-878542-24-9. *Topics: meeting basics, leader and participant behaviors, the meeting process, making meetings work.*

People Skills

How To Deal With Difficult People, Paul Friedman. SkillPath Publications, Inc., 1991. ISBN 1-878542-03-6. *Topics: what makes people difficult, changing difficult behaviors, difficulties, being the solution – not the problem, difficult modes of talk, encouraging desirable behavior.*

Rules For Reaching Consensus, Steven Saint & James R. Lawson. Jossey-Bass Pfeiffer, 1994. ISBN 0-89384-256-7. *Topics: collective decision-making, overview of consensus meeting, preconsensus process, rules, tips for facilitators.*

Dealing With Difficult Participants, Bob Pike & Dave Arch. Jossey-Bass Pfeiffer, 1997. ISBN 0-7879-1116-X. *Topics: latecomer, preoccupied, cell phones & beepers, introvert, domineering, skeptic.*

(continued)

People Skills (continued)

How To Read A Person Like A Book, Gerald I. Nierenberg & Henry H. Calero. Pocket Books, 1971. ISBN 0-671-73557-8. *Topics: reading gestures, facial expressions, walking gestures, openness, defensiveness.*

Body Language, Julius Fast. Pocket Books - Simon & Schuster Inc., 1970. ISBN 0-671-67325-4. *Topics: what your posture says, movement & the message, postures & presentations.*

Flipchart & Visual Tools

Flip Chart Power – Secrets of the Masters, Bonnie E. Burn. Jossey-Bass Pfeiffer, 1996. ISBN 0-88390-485-3. *Topics: using flip charts, making flip charts, presenting flip charts, other presentation tools, whiteboard & chalkboard use, slide use, videotape use.*

A Picture's Worth 1000 Words – A Workbook For Visual Communications, Jean Westcott & Jennifer Hammond Landau. Jossey-Bass Pfeiffer, 1997. ISBN 0-7879-0352-3. *Topics: lettering, basic shapes, cartoon faces, arrows, people, color, applications.*

The Big Book Of Flip Charts, Robert William Lucas. McGraw Hill, 2000. ISBN 0-07-134311-3. *Topics: basic layout & design principles, balance, using color, writing legibly, looking professional at the easel, techniques for facilitating meetings.*

Flip Charts - How to Draw Them and How to Use Them, Richard C. Brandt. Pfeiffer & Company, 1986. ISBN 0-88390-031-9. *Topics: basics of using flip charts, markers, printing, color, balance & symmetry, transportation, storage.*

Facilitation Skills

The Facilitator's Fieldbook, Tom Justice & David W. Jamieson. HRD Press, Inc., 1999. ISBN 0-8144-7038-6. *Topics: organizing the group, group norms, planning meetings, decision modes, handling conflicts, evaluation and group closure.*

Facilitator's Guide to Participatory Decision-Making, Sam Kaner. New Society Publishers, 1998. ISBN 0-86571-347-2. *Topics: grounding principles, facilitator fundamentals, building sustainable agreements.*

(continued)

Facilitation Skills (continued)

Facilitation: From Discussion to Decision, A.L. Zimmerman & Carol J. Evans. Nichols Publishing, 1993. ISBN 0-89397-419-6. *Topics: strategies, skills, preparation, psychological background, climate, synergy, terms, feedback*

Facilitation Skills For Team Leaders, Donald Hackett, Charles L. Martin. Crisp Publications, Inc., 1993. ISBN 0-56052-199-6. *Topics: understanding facilitation, team involvement, decision making, dynamics, facilitation tools, crossword facilitation.*

Facilitating With Ease, Ingrid Bens. Jossey-Bass, Inc., 2000. ISBN 0-7879-5194-3. *Topics: understanding facilitation, facilitation stages, knowing your participants, creating participation, facilitating conflict, effective decision making, meeting management, process tools for facilitators, process designs.*

The ASTD Trainer's Sourcebook: Facilitation Skills, Dennis Kinlaw. McGraw-Hill, 1996. ISBN 0-07-053444-6. *Topics: model for superior facilitation, quality communication, special functions of facilitation, rational tools, assessment tools, visual aids.*

The Facilitator Excellence Handbook, Fran Rees. Jossey-Bass Pfeiffer, 1998. ISBN 0-7879-3888-2. *Topics: benefits of facilitation, verbal techniques, nonverbal techniques, recording techniques, reading the group, facilitating consensus, ranking & evaluating material, designing facilitation, levels of facilitation competency, managing yourself.*

How To Lead Work Teams, Fran Rees. Jossey-Bass Pfeiffer, 2001. ISBN 0-7879-5691-0. *Topics: values-based facilitation, facilitating productive team communication, facilitating team meetings, encouraging participation, recording people's ideas, managing group process.*

The Compleat Facilitator: A Guide, Barry J. Roberts & Kevin Upton. Howick Associates, 1994. ISBN 0-9646972-0-3. *Topics: role of the facilitator, meeting management, problem solving, dealing with people.*

The Art of Facilitation – How To Create Group Synergy, Dale Hunter, Anne Bailey & Bill Taylor. Fisher Books, 1995. ISBN 1-55561-101-X. *Topics: facilitation basics, workshop design, facilitative processes, uncovering sabotage patterns.*

The Facilitators' Handbook, John Heron. Kogan Page, Ltd., 1994. ISBN 0-7494-0010-2. *Topics: group dynamics, planning, confrontation, facilitator style.*

(continued)

Facilitation Skills (continued)

Facilitation – Providing Opportunities for Learning, Trevor Bentley. McGraw-Hill International (UK), Ltd., 1994. ISBN 0-07-707684-2. *Topics: working with groups, facilitation skills, intervention strategies, managing interaction.*

Masterful Facilitation, A. Glenn Kiser. American Management Association, 1998. ISBN 0-8144-0398-0. *Topics: facilitation model, making initial contact, designing the intervention, evaluating the results, working with a cofacilitator.*

The Facilitator's Toolkit, Lynn Kearny. HRD Press, Inc., 1995. ISBN 0-87425-268-7. *Topics: creative thinking with groups, facilitation map, six basic group needs, managing the process.*

The Facilitation Skills Training Kit, Leslie Bendaly. McGraw-Hill, 2000. ISBN 0-07-134734-8. *Topics: group process facilitation skills, basic responsibilities of the facilitator, techniques for generating, collecting and organizing ideas, dealing with difficult behaviors, decision making tools, creating dialogue, reaching consensus, structured problem solving, team facilitation skills.*

Faultless Facilitation: A Resource Guide for Group and Team Leaders, Lois B. Hart. HRD Press, Inc., 1992. ISBN 0-97425-167-2. *Topics: understanding leadership and facilitation, getting off on the right foot, warming up the group, unspoken messages, clarifying and ranking problems, visual aids.*

Learning Programs

Interaction Associates, Inc.
600 Townsend Street, Suite 550
San Francisco, CA 94103
(415) 241-8000
IA is a consulting firm specializing in real-life facilitation. They offer courses in Facilitative Leadership, Mastering Meetings, and Facilitating Change. They also offer a week-long "Facilitator Institute" that teaches people how to use their "Interaction Method."

"To know what is possible tomorrow you must be willing to step outside of what is possible today. The long view is all."

— **Toshiba advertisement**

> "The most valuable gift you can give another is a good example."
> — **B. Bader**

23 EXAMPLES YOU CAN USE

Here are some examples that will help you. Please feel free to copy the examples in this chapter — make your own flipcharts and use them in your sessions!

You'll also find other examples of documents and signs that will help you in any of your facilitation sessions.

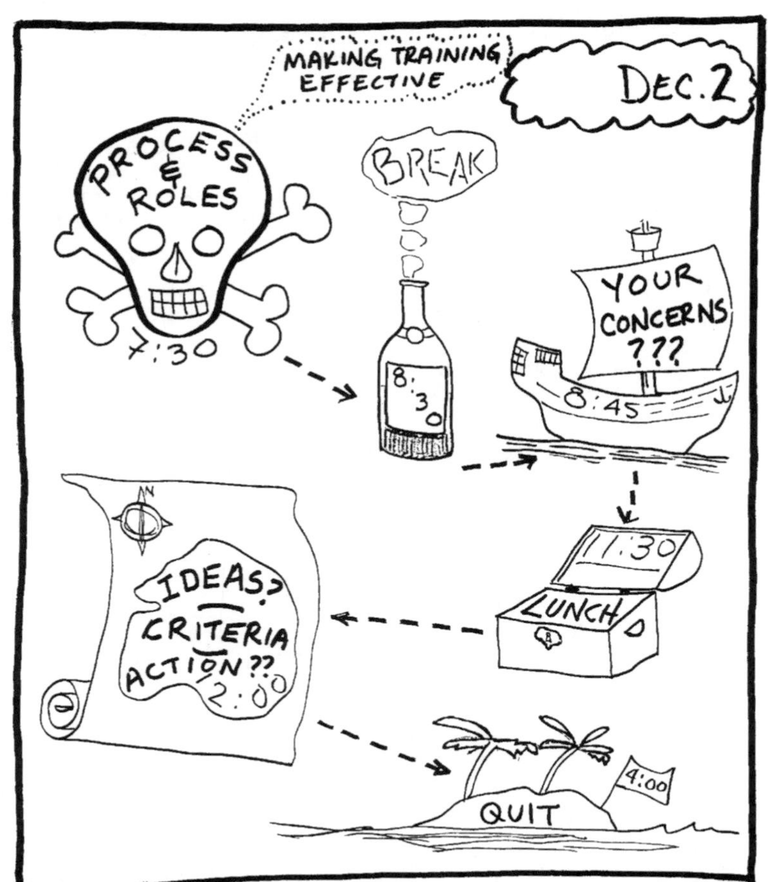

Agenda — fun

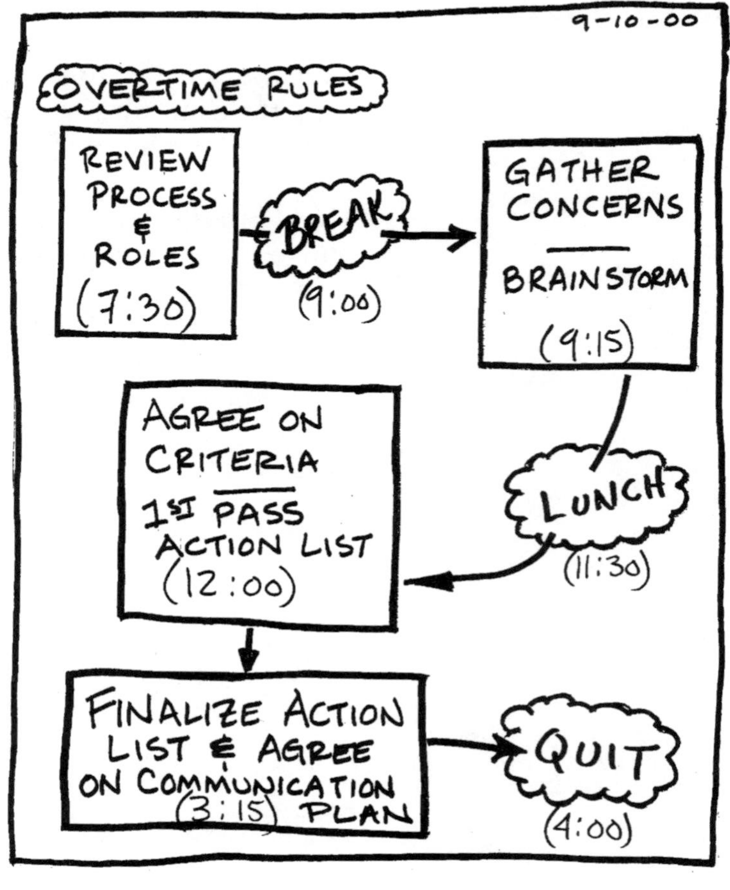

Agenda — flow diagram

Agenda — road signs

PAYROLL ISSUE

AGENDA

9-26-01

- REVIEW AGENDA
- RULES - ROLES - PROCESS
- REVIEW CONCERNS
- POSSIBLE ACTIONS?
- BUILD CRITERIA LIST
- NEXT STEP?

QUIT @ 6:00 p.m.

Agenda — list style

Agenda — fun

Agenda — balloons

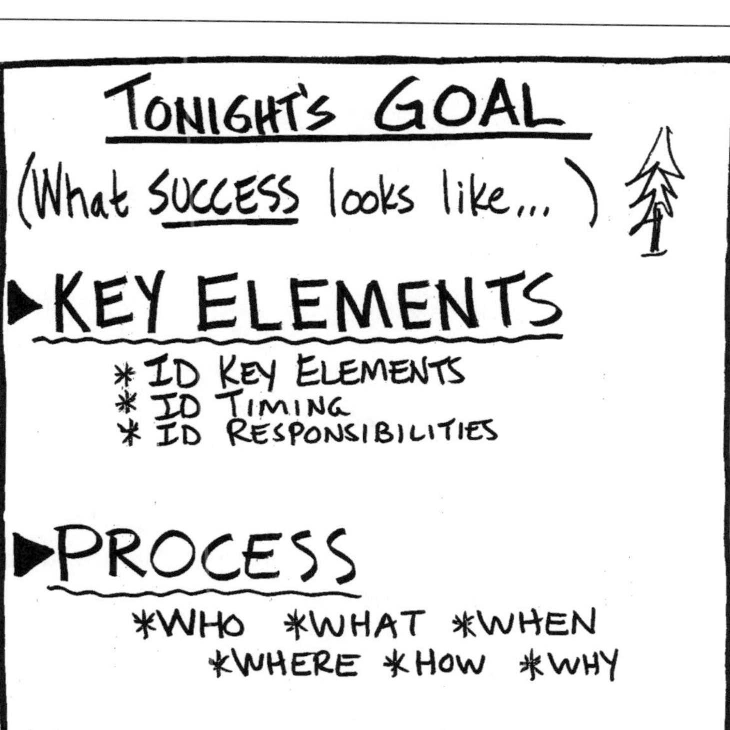

Tonight's Goal — Prepared before the meeting by the facilitator. Used to visually outline key steps for the meeting.

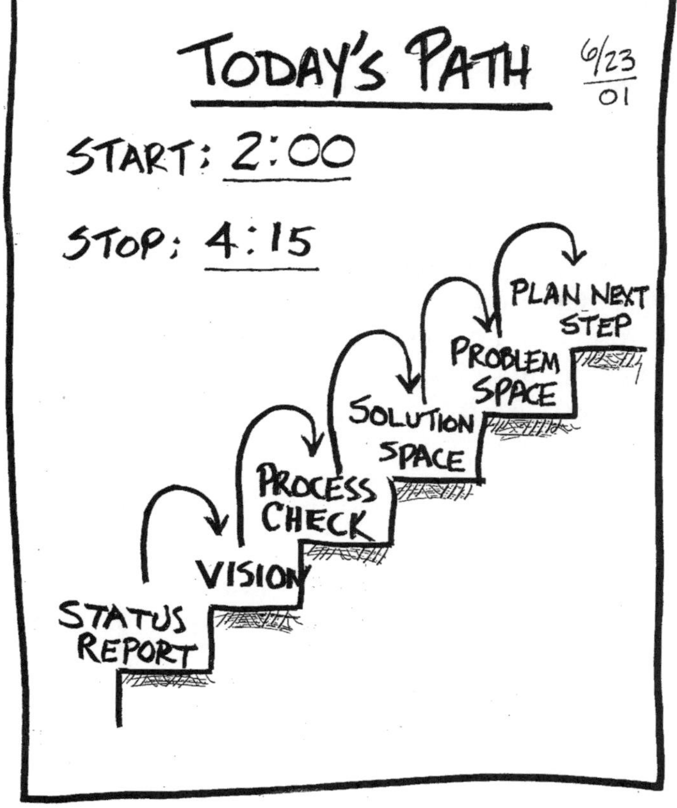

Agenda — steps

News Bin
— Prepared before the meeting by the facilitator. Used to record reports or news contributed by participants during a "sharing time" in the session.

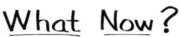

Process Check
— Created by the facilitator during break time. Use to poll the group members on what step they'd like to do next.

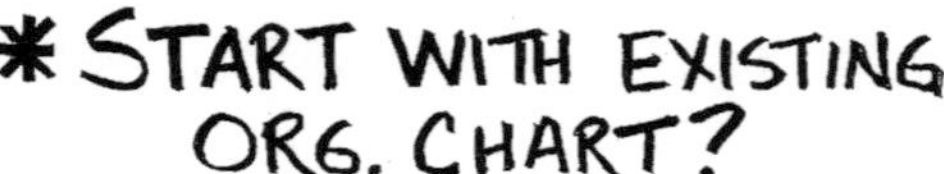

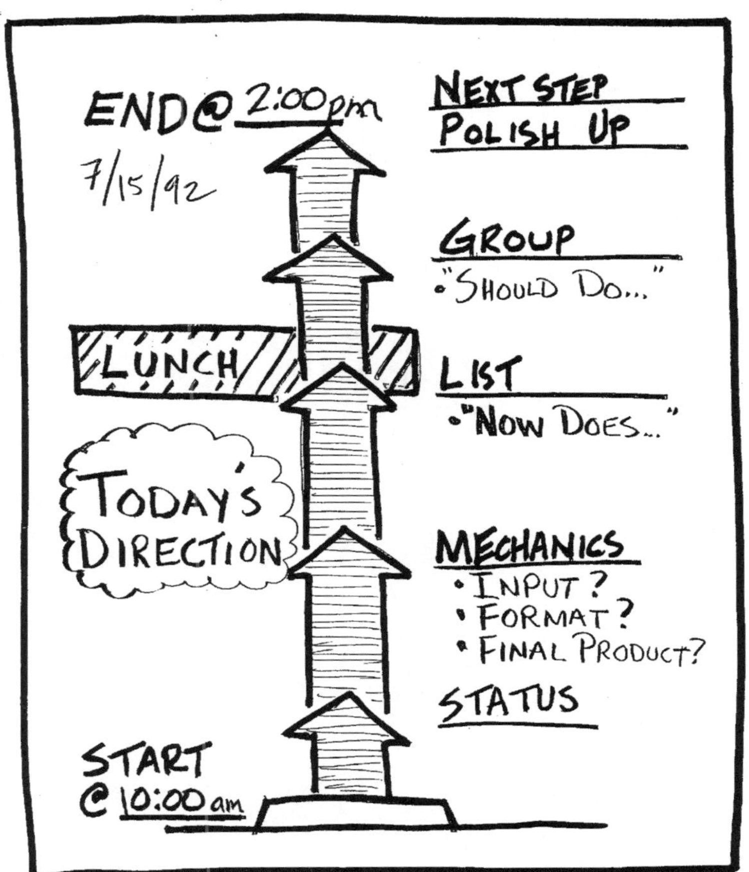

Agenda — upward arrow

List of Benefits
— List of ideas generated by the group. Used to focus the group members on the value of the facilitation session.

List of BENEFITS 2/26/01

1. ALLOWS US TO GET AQQUAINTED
2. ABILITY TO SHARE COMMUNION IN VARIOUS FORMS
3. WORSHIP GOD TOGETHER AS SINGLE GROUP
4. OUTWARD SIGN OF WHAT SAY WE ARE...
5. "SELLING POINT" TO OTHERS IN COMMUNITY
6. IT'S UNIQUE

ISSUE: OVERTIME RULES

OUR AGREEMENTS

9-10/00

1) IT'S OK IF PEOPLE ARE NOT SUPPORTIVE

2) DISRUPTIVE BEHAVIOR= NOT OK

3) WE'LL COMMUNICATE OUR SCHEDULES TO ALLOW OTHER TRAINERS TO LEARN FROM OUR PRESENTATIONS

Our agreements
— A group-generated list of behavior agreements.

POSSIBILITIES

5-25/00

- BE AN EXPERT ON A FEW MODULES
- HAVE SEVERAL EXPERTS ON EACH MODULE
- EVERYONE IS AN EXPERT ON THE FIRST FOUR MODULES
- BE A GENERALIST WITH YOUR CREW

FIRST, EVERYONE TEACHES FIRST 4 MODULES

Possibilities
— A short list of possible actions generated by the group.

12-8/97 "TO DO" LIST ①

TASK	WHO?	BY WHEN?
PREPARE INSTRUCTIONS FOR HANDLING $ FOR FOOD, ETC.	GBP/DW	12/15
PREPARE INFORMATION PACKET ON 20 MODULES FOR LEADERS	Ken D.	JAN 5
NEED A MEETING TO MAKE CLEAR ROLES & RESPONSIBILITIES FOR TEAM SKILLS TRAINING	DAVE & LANCE	JAN 5
TEACH AS MANY OF 1ST FOUR MODULES	ALL	FEB 1
MEET AGAIN - ISSUES - FEEDBACK	ALL	FEB 2

To Do List
— The classic action litem list showing the what, who, and when. Generated by the group at the end of the meeting.

12-8/97 TIME SCHEDULE

MONTH	ACTIVITY
DEC '97	• FACIL. SESSION - TUES/WED • MTG W/ STAKEHOLDERS
JAN '98	• HBO LEADERS' SKILLS (3) - JAN. 12 • REVIEW MTG W/ MGMNT TEAM • LOOK AT ACTION LIST
FEB '98	• HBO LEADERS' SKILLS (2) • REDESIGN TEAM (8EE) AND WEEKLY MTGS (40EE) • REVIEW ACTION ITEMS
MAR '98	• GATHER FEEDBACK • FACIL. SESSION MTG - MAR 6 (CHECK PROGRESS)

Time Schedule
— A valuable tool for showing tasks over a long-term schedule. Format (month & activity blocks) are drawn by the facilitator before the meeting. Activity blocks are then filled in by the group during the session.

ISSUE BIN

11-2/00

- REVISIT OUR VISION?
- WHAT HAPPENED TO THE UM? (UNION INVOLVEMENT IN THE "PROCESS"?)
- NEED TO PUSH THE "D" DOWN
- UNLOADING THE PROCESS COUNCIL
  - ROLE - EXPECTATIONS
- MORE COMMUNICATIONS FROM COUNCILS TO THE EMPLOYEES
- START WITH EASY TOPIC/ISSUES – LEARN THE PROCESS.

Issue Bin
— A helpful tool to hold ideas or comments that could otherwise disrupt the flow of the process. The facilitator or scribe records the participant's input and keeps the process ontrack without discussion delays.

Plus/Delta Feedback
— Used by the facilitator to gather group feedback on the process. This sheet is always one of the last steps in the process. The facilitator asks the group, "What did you like about this process?" and "What could we do better next time?"

8-16/01

+	Δ
- LOTS OF PEOPLE ATTENDED	- HAVE REST OF RLGX ATTEND
- CONTINUE MTG	- SOFT CHAIR FOR BURTSIS
- ROOM, FOOD	- NO DOTS
- COVERAGE FOR SHIFT EMPLOYEES	- BRING SUCCESSES TO SHARE
- PROFESSIONAL BEHAVIOR²	- PERSONAL CHOICE SEATING
- HONEST, OPEN	- USE CONSENSUS TOOLS
- 3 MIN. SHARING	- ACCOMPLISH SOMETHING
- FACIL. HELP	- CLEARER/DEFINITIVE "NEXT STEPS"
- JULIE H. ATTENDANCE	- ACCOMPLISH OUR OBJECTIVE(S)
- I'M STILL AFLOAT!	

Welcome Sign
— Prepared before the meeting. Used to create eustress, a positive atmosphere, in the meeting. Having a welcome sign is very important. This is an opportunity for the facilitator to be creative and colorful.

Authority Level Question
— This flipchart is used in first meeting to determine the group's authority level. The classic question used is, "Who has the D?" (who has the authority to make decisions?).

4-14-00

SHARING TIME

PURPOSE

GIVE EVERYONE A CHANCE TO TELL US WHAT'S ON YOUR MIND.

EXAMPLES

- WHAT'S GOING WELL?
- WHAT'S NOT GOING SO WELL
- FEELINGS
- OBSERVATIONS
- DEEP THOUGHTS

Sharing Time
— A great ice breaker! The facilitator prepares this flipchart before the first meeting to help participants open up and start talking. It is very important to explain the purpose and rules of the exercise, as well as give examples.

SHARING TIME ②

5-30-99

RULES

- 3 MINUTES EACH
- 5 MINUTES PREPARATION (FOR ALL) @ BEGINNING

RULES for Sharing Time

- Keep it **professional** and not personal
- Attack problems, not people
- No questions until all have shared
- OK to disagree but not be disagreeable
- 3 minutes maximum time per person
- No criticism of other person's comments
- OK to pass

- DECISION OF TIME KEEPER ARE FINAL. PERIOD

Seperate People From The Problem!

Focus on Interests Not Positions!

Invent Options For Mutual Gain!

Insist On Using Objective Criteria!

2-1/01 ↑ Special Guidelines ↑

Special Guidelines
— After several hours of working the process, this flipchart was created by one of the participants during a break. Its purpose was to help the group move ahead in the process by spelling-out a special set of behavioral guidelines. The facilitator used this flipchart as a proposal and reviewed it with the group to get its support for them.

4/1/99

Guidelines

No Group Judging or Criticism

1. Review List - Clarify
2. Add to List
3. You [Criteria] Pick Top 1/3 - Priority
4. Deadlines for Top 1/3

Guidelines
— Used for a "second look" at possibilities generated at the prior meeting and steps to reduce their number by selecting the top one-third. A guideline flipchart like this is an excellent visual tool for bringing the group back to the same starting place in a new meeting.

What Do We Need To Do? — A graphic tool used by the facilitator to prompt discussion within the group. This tool is helpful when a group become stagnate or deadlocked.

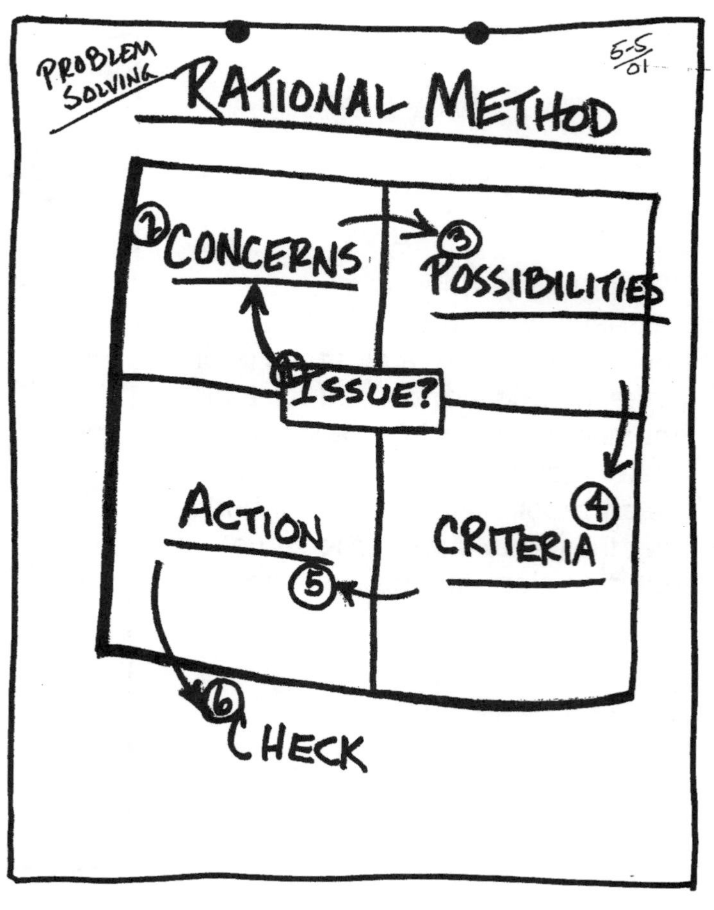

The Rational Method — Used by the facilitator to explain the six step problem solving process to participants during the first meeting.

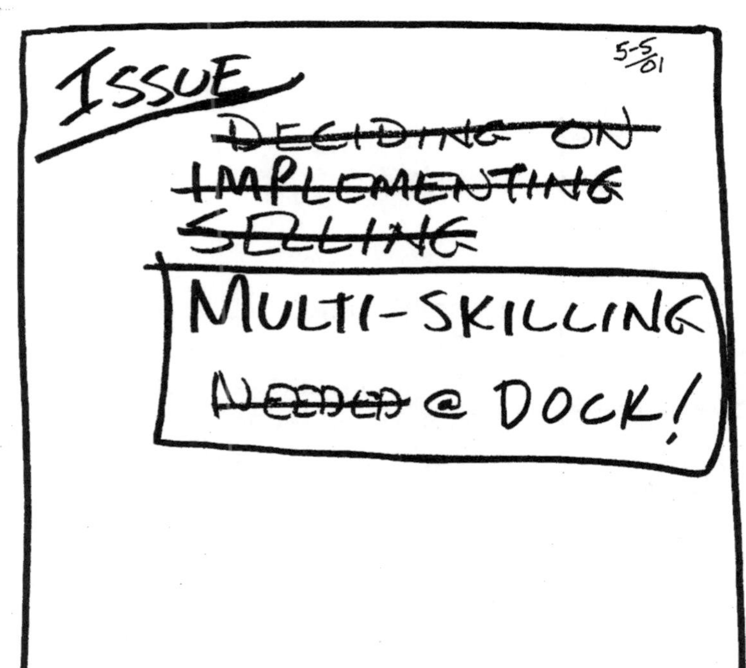

Issue
— A good example of how the facilitator used the flipchart to cross-out and change the proposed issue until the group could support the final version (the text in the box is the issue ultimately supported by the entire group).

Boundaries
— This list of boundaries and group constraints was presented by the leader to the group at the first meeting. The flipchart was drawn by the facilitator before the meeting—based on information gathered at an earlier meeting between the facilitator and the leader.

6-19/00

BOUNDARIES

- SKILL MUST BE APPLIED
- PAY SUBJECT TO RLQ APPROVAL
- JUSTIFIED BY BUSINESS CASE – -HOW WILL IT IMPROVE "BOTTOM LINE"?
- OVERALL PAYROLL MUST ↓
- CHOICE: MULTI-SKILL OR/ RECOGNITION PROGRAM
- CAN HAVE MS OR RECOGNITION AND SUCCESS SHARING – BUT NOT ALL
- MEMO: THINGS WILL BE ASSIGNED THAT ARE NOT PART OF MULTI-SKILLING (TBD)

POSSIBILITIES ①

6/19/00

- BUDGET THE MONEY FOR TRNG
- TAKE EXISTING MAT'L & "COMPLETE" THEM
- DO IT ON ONE SEGMENT
- DO IT FOR ENTIRE
- "SHOOT IT" – DO ~~ANY~~ AWAY w/ IT
- DO SOMETHING w/ SUCCESS-SHARING INSTEAD M.S.
- MAKE LOCAL RECOG. MORE "LINE-OF-SIGHT" TO SUPPORT M.S.
- DO EVALUATION OF NEEDS (FOR TODAY)
- OPEN NEG. & REWRITE JOB DESC. w/ PAY
- HIRE CONSULTANT
- MOVE ALL TO CEO PAY LEVEL & DO WHAT WE WANT
- ADJUST OUR PAY LEVELS

Possibilities
— Brainstormed by the group. Note the mistakes and crossed-out words. When recording brainstormed ideas, don't worry about getting the words perfect or clean. Keep the momentum going in the brainstorming by not getting bogged-down with spelling or organization concerns.

5-5/99

CRITERIA FOR PRIORITY ITEMS

① LEGAL & MORALE & SAFE
② MOVES US "AHEAD" – BENEFIT TO CO. AND EMPLOYEES
③ ABIDES BY UNION CONTRACT
④ CONSISTENT w/ COMPANY POLICIES
⑤ RECOGNIZES RESOURCES ~~AVAIL~~ AVAIL.

Criteria
— A short list of criteria generated by the group.

CONCERNS

6-19-00

①

- OTHERS DOING IT W/O PAY
- SYSTEM IS TOO COMPLICATED
- THERE'S BIG GAP BETWEEN MGMNT & O/M ON $ EXPECTATIONS
- TIME REQ'D TO ADMIN. CHANGE
- "ALL-AT-ONCE" CONCEPT
- DIFFERENCE: "APPLIED SKILLS" VS, "LEARNED" SKILLS
- MULTI-SKILLING VS/ NEED TO DO BASE JOB
- HAVE TIME/RESOURCES NOW TO DO?
- HAVE RIGHT AMOUNT OF PEOPLE?
- SAFETY FACTORS BUILT-IN??
- DESIRE OF PEOPLE TO DO IT

Concerns
— Two pages of concerns generated by a group. Note the use of abbreviations and symbols by the recorder (or facilitator) to save time and minimize the time "turning your back to the group."

6-19-00

CONCERNS

- PREFERENTIAL TREATMENT
- A LOT WORK ALREADY – WASTE OF TIME NOW
- MAKE SURE WHO HAS "D" ON THIS (QRM VS, RMM OK)
- LEVEL OF IMPACT FOR ALL THE WORK
- DRAG IT THRU MUD (AGAIN) FOR YRS
- ALREADY HAVE PAY SCHED. & JOB DESCRIP.
- PROMISES GIVEN (FOR M.S.) IN FIRST PLACE
- WHY APPROACH IT ORIGINALLY AND CAN IT BE ACCOM. NOW – POSITIVE?
- TRAINING!
- IF WE GIVE UP ON THIS – MIGHT AS WELL NOT DO ANYTHING. WADDA WE GOIN DO?
- POSSIBLE "IMBALANCE" – SO MUCH ON BASIC JOB NOW – NO OPPORT. FOR M.S.
- NO PAY W/ M.S.

11-1/00

ACTION ITEMS

WHAT?	WHO?	BY WHEN?
WRITE JOB DESCRIPTION	ROY	11-29/00
HIRE CONSULTANT	RICK	12-25/00
INCR. PAY FOR OO BY 50¢/hr for M.S.		

Action Items
— Keep it simple: what, who, and when.

The Next Step
— Always the forgotten step by the group. Participants are so anxious to get out of the meeting that they forget to plan for the next steps. It is the facilitator's responsibility to complete this step before participants escape.

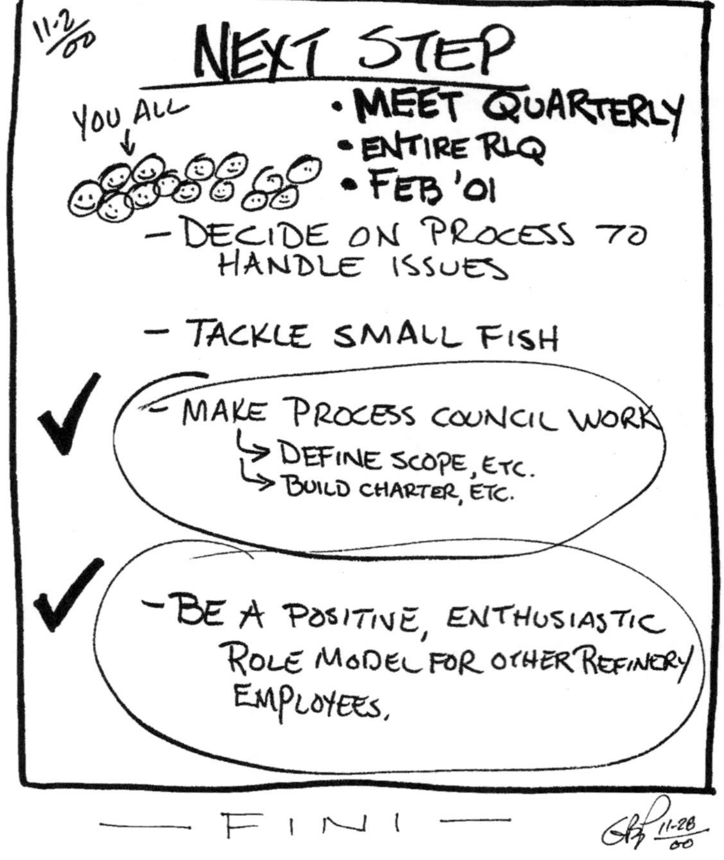

11-2/00
NEXT STEP
YOU ALL
• MEET QUARTERLY
• ENTIRE RLQ
• FEB '01
– DECIDE ON PROCESS TO HANDLE ISSUES
– TACKLE SMALL FISH
– MAKE PROCESS COUNCIL WORK
↳ DEFINE SCOPE, ETC.
↳ BUILD CHARTER, ETC.
– BE A POSITIVE, ENTHUSIASTIC ROLE MODEL FOR OTHER REFINERY EMPLOYEES.

— FINI —

11-28/00

4-21-00

CRITERIA

{MULTI-SKILLING}

WHATEVER WE DO, IT WILL...

- BE LEGAL & MORAL
- COMPLY WITH COMPANY POLICIES
- COMPLY WITH CURRENT LABOR CONTRACT
- PAYROLL MUST ↓
- UTILIZE APPLIED SKILLS
- SUPPORTS SAFETY AND CONTINUES OUR FINE RECORD

Criteria

— Another example of criteria generated by a group.

More Ground Rules

1. Accept mistakes in good faith.
2. Titles & positions will be left at the door.
3. Treat each other with respect.
4. Stick to any agreements made.
5. Relax & enjoy the meeting
6. Let people finish talking – don't interrupt!
7. OK to say "Pass" for your turn.
8. One "war story" per person per mtg.
9. We will make decisions together based on consensus.
10. Active listening & active participation
11. No phone calls – no cell phones.
12. Be supportive – not judgmental!

October 31, 2001

November 29 & 30
Problem Solving Session:
Food Selection At The Cafeteria

Rodney Bryan
Arturo Bulgesse
John Otting
Bob Strahorn
Helge Hansen
Davis Jefferson
Bernard Bear
Christina Holmquist
Rodney Augustus

Congratulations!

You are invited to a problem solving meeting on Wednesday and Thursday, November 29 & 30. This is the seventh year that we conducted this process to improve food quality at our cafeteria.

Employees who have participated in this facilitated process have been able to improve food quality in our plant. Our experiences shows that facilitated groups have a better focus on the issue, are more creative in their solutions, and have greater group support for action they take.

The objective of this session is to give you the knowledge and tools necessary to understand and solve our ongoing food quality problems. Since this year will probably see more High Performance Organization (HPO) related activities, you will likely be called upon to facilitate similar problem-solving groups within your department. Such team facilitations will be critical as we review other group work processes and problems within our company.

Our sessions will be held in the Solid Fuel Terminal conference room. The sessions begin promptly at 8:00 a.m. and ends no later than 5:00 p.m. I will be your facilitator for the entire process.

Since this group is small, we are counting on your attendance. If you cannot attend this session, please notify me immediately. We have a waiting list of employees who would like to participate in this problem solving process.

If you have any questions, please contact me at work (555-1212) or at my home (555-1313).

We look forward to seeing you on Wednesday morning!

G. B. Putz

WELCOME LETTER: One-Month Before First Meeting

Guidelines for Reaching Consensus

1 Avoid arguing for your own individual judgments. Approach the task on the basis of **logic**.

2 Avoid changing your mind if it is **only to reach agreement** and avoid conflict. Support only solutions with which you are able to agree at least somewhat.

3 Avoid "conflict-reducing" techniques such as majority **vote**, averaging, or trading when reaching your decision.

4 View differences of opinion as a **help** rather than a hindrance in decision-making.

WALL CHART

> "The great end of life in not knowledge but action."
> — **T.H. Huxley**

INDEX

A

Accommodation 16-2
Acid test for consensus 15-2
Action
- case study 8-3
- example flipchart 23-22
- introduction 8-1
- typical flipcharts 8-5
- use of criteria 8-6
- what to do 8-2

Agenda, example flipchart 23-2, -3, -4, -5, -7
Alice & Cheshire Cat 4-5
AOPBAOS 4-8
Arbitration 1-5
Attackers 16-5
Attitude, importance 20-7
Authority level
- "C" 11-5, 11-6
- "D" 11-5, 11-6
- example flipchart 23-11
- "I" 11-5, 11-6
- overview 11-4

Autocratic decision making 8-6
Avoidance 16-2

B

Bargaining 1-5
Behavior
- attack 16-10
- chaos 16-10
- interpersonal 16-10
- lonesome warrior 16-10
- mob 16-10
- passive 16-10
- passive-aggressive 16-8
- difficult 16-7

Behaviors
- functional 16-8
- problem 16-5

Benefits
- consensus 15-3
- example flipchart 23-7

Berkeley i-7
Books
- facilitation skills 22-3, -4, -5
- flipcharts 22-3
- meeting skills 22-2
- people skills 22-2

Boundaries, example flipchart 23-15
Brainstorming
- case study 6-6
- dry spells 6-3, 6-9
- example flipchart 23-8, 23-16
- having silence 6-3, 6-8, 6-9
- introduction 6-2
- right & left brains 6-3
- rules 6-5
- types 6-4

Broken records 16-5
Brownout 19-4
Burnout 19-4

C

"C" authority level 11-5, 11-6
Caroline i-13, 12-2
Carroll, Lewis 4-5
Case study
- action 8-3
- brainstorming 6-6
- check 9-7
- criteria 7-5

Check
- actions & concerns 9-2
- case study 9-7
- communications plan 9-6
- details 9-8, 9-9
- for desired outcomes 9-4
- introduction 9-1
- next step? 9-5
- why do one? 9-3

Cheshire Cat 4-5
Cluster diagrams 13-2
Collaboration
- general 1-6, 1-7, 16-2
- benefits of 1-7

Colors
- passion created 13-4, 13-5
- use by facilitator 13-4, 13-5

Communications
- ideas 9-6
- misfires 19-4
- plan 9-6

Competition 16-2
Concerns
- and solutions 5-6
- case study 5-3
- example flipchart 23-17
- gathering 5-2, 5-5
- introduction 5-1

Conflict
- accommodation 16-2
- approaches 16-2
- avoidance 16-2
- collaboration 16-2
- competition 16-2
- constructive 16-3
- destructive 16-3
- disruptions 16-4
- how to handle 16-4
- introduction 16-1
- problem behaviors 16-5
- types 16-1

Consensus
- acid test for 15-2
- benefits 15-3
- example flipchart 23-22
- fist or five 15-6
- for action items 8-6
- guidelines for reaching 15-4, 15-8
- introduction 15-1
- negative voting 15-5
- straw-voting 15-5
- toolbox 15-5
- voting 15-4, 21-7

Content 2-6

Criteria
- advanced 7-3
- basic 7-2
- case study 7-5
- creating 7-4
- example flipchart 23-16, 23-19
- general & specific 7-8
- introduction 7-1

Customer service teams 1-8

D

"D" authority level 11-5, 11-6

Danielle i-13, 12-2

Decisions
- autocratic style 8-6
- choices 15-2
- democratic style 8-6
- styles 8-6
- unanimous style 8-6

Democratic decision making 8-6

Desired outcomes, checking for 9-4

Diagrams 13-2

Difficult behaviors 16-7

Disney Institute i-7

Disruptions, handling 16-4, 16-11

Drawings 13-2

Dry spells 6-3, 6-9

Duck hunters 10-5, 21-3

E

East Beach i-7

Ethical issues 2-7

Example flipcharts
- action items 23-9, 23-18
- agenda 23-2, -3, -4, -5, -7
- agreements 23-8
- authority level 23-11
- benefits list 23-7
- boundaries 23-15
- concerns 23-17
- consensus guidelines 23-22
- criteria 23-16, 23-19
- feedback 23-10
- ground rules 23-20
- guidelines 23-13
- issue 23-15
- issue bin 23-10
- need to do 23-14
- news bin 23-6
- next step 23-18
- plus/delta 23-10
- possibilities 23-8, 23-16
- process check 23-6
- process steps 23-15
- rational method 23-14
- sharing time 23-12
- time schedule 23-9
- to do list 23-9
- welcome 23-11
- welcome letter 23-21

Examples 23-1

F

Facilitation Process 1-1

Facilitation
- alternatives to 1-5
- is and is not 1-8
- key elements for success 1-2
- other challenges 2-9
- selling the benefits 14-2
- six steps 1-3
- the Bigger Picture 1-4
- training classes 22-5
- use of humor 2-10

Facilitator
- content owner 2-6
- desired behaviors 2-5
- ethical issues 2-7
- job of 2-1, 2-4
- maintaining positive climate 2-9
- neutral 21-4
- outside of control 17-8
- process owner 2-6
- pushing & pulling 2-3
- role 2-2
- things to do 2-10
- trip wires 2-8

FAQs 21-1
Feedback 23-10
First meeting
- advanced ground rules 14-6
- agenda 14-3
- basic ground rules 14-5
- important points to cover 14-8
- introduction 14-1, 14-9
- issue bin 14-10
- pre-meeting logistics 12-1
- roadmap to it 10-4
- stakeholders 10-5

Fist or five 15-7
Five Whys 17-7
Flipcharts
- books 22-3, 22-4, 22-5
- graphics 13-6
- hanger 3-2, 3-3
- introduction 13-1
- making interesting 13-7
- management 13-8
- pre-meeting preparation 21-5
- tearing sheets 13-8

Forming 20-6
Free-wheeling 6-4
Functional behaviors 16-8

G

Geese, lessons from 3-6
General criteria 7-8
Getting started
- introduction 10-1
- steps 10-3

Green, Dennis i-13
Grids 13-2
Ground rules
- advanced 14-6
- basic 14-5
- example flipchart 23-20

H

Hammond's Beach i-7
Headshakers 16-5
Hints
- don't do 20-2
- helpful 20-4
- to do 20-3, 20-5

I

"I" authority level 11-5, 11-6
Incident investigations 1-8
Inclusive work environment 17-6, 17-8, 17-9
Interaction Associates Inc. 22-5
Interventions 16-6
Issue bin
- example flipchart 23-10
- use 14-10

Issue
- case study 4-3
- dangers of assumption 4-7
- example flipchart 23-15
- introduction 4-1
- more that one 4-2
- not action statement 4-6
- procedure to determine 4-4
- statement 4-6
- what's the? 4-2

K

Kindness trap 5-6

L

Last, Curt i-13
Latecomers 16-5
Leader
- and you 11-1
- as facilitator 21-2
- behavior 21-6
- worksheet 11-3

Lists 13-2
Logistics 12-1
Logistics Manager 3-2, 3-3
Loudmouths 16-5

M

Mediation 1-5
Meetings
- first one 14-1
- length 21-3
- skills 22-2
- why they fail 14-2

Miramar Beach i-7

N

Negative voting 15-5
Negotiation 1-5
News bin 23-6
Newton, Jim i-13
Norming 20-6

O

Over-communication 10-6

P

Paine, Thomas 1-1
Paper method 6-4
Participants
- role of 3-1, 3-9
- role Q&A 3-8
- task roles 3-2

Participation
- benefits of 17-2
- facilitator control 17-8
- facilitator's behaviors 17-1
- inclusive environment 17-6
- keep it moving 17-5, 17-7
- motivating 17-6
- risk-free environment 17-4
- ways to promote 17-3

Passive-aggressive
- definition 16-8
- examples 16-8

People skills 22-2
Perceived equity 17-8
Performing 20-6
Positive atmosphere 17-4
Positive climate 2-9
Possibilities
- example flipchart 23-8, 23-16
- introduction 6-1

Posters 13-2
Pre-meeting
- logistics 12-1
- welcome letter 12-2, 12-3

Process
- agreement example flipchart 23-8
- check example flipchart 23-6
- concept 2-6
- example flipchart 23-14, 23-15
- guidelines example flipchart 23-13
- need-to-do example flipchart 23-14
- next step example flipchart 23-18
- roles 3-4, 3-5, 3-9
- sharing time example flipchart 23-12
- to-do example flipchart 23-9

Pushing & pulling 2-3

Q

Questions, frequently asked ones 21-1

R

Rational method 23-14
Recorder 3-2, 3-3, 13-10
Reed people 10-5, 21-3
Resources 22-1
Risk-free environment 17-4
Roadmap, to first meeting 10-4

Role
- flipchart hanger 3-2, 3-3
- logistics manager 3-2, 3-3
- recorder 3-2, 3-3, 13-10
- scribe 3-2, 3-3, 3-8
- timekeeper 3-2, 3-3

Room, set up 12-5, 12-6
Round robin 6-4
Rules, brainstorming 6-5

S

Santa Barbara i-7
Scribe 3-2, 3-3, 3-8, 21-2
Sigma Nu i-7
Silence hurdle 6-8
Solutions
- and concerns 5-6
- possible 6-1

Spaces, opening & closing 1-4
Specific criteria 7-8
Stakeholders 10-5
Storming 20-6
Strategic moment 21-6
Straw voting 15-5
Stress
- avoiding 19-5
- danger signs 19-4
- handling 19-3
- indicators 19-2
- managing 19-1
- recognizing 19-2
- rethinking 19-2
- saying "no" 19-6

Suzie i-13, 12-2
Synergy 17-2

T

Task roles 3-2
Team formation steps 20-6
Tearing flipchart sheets 13-8
Time schedule 23-9
Timekeeper 3-2, 3-3
Toolbox for consensus 15-5
Tough situations 16-7, 16-8, 16-9
Training classes 22-5
Trip wires 2-8
Trust
- attributes 18-3
- building 18-1
- busters 18-2
- facilitator's behaviors 18-5, 18-7
- groups lacking it 18-3
- key elements 18-4
- specific actions 18-6

Tuolumne River i-7

U

Unanimous decision making 8-6

V

Visual tools
- cluster diagrams 13-2
- colors 13-4, 13-5
- create emotions 13-6
- diagrams 13-2
- drawings 13-2
- grids 13-2
- introduction 13-1
- lists 13-2
- posters 13-2
- toolkit 13-3
- types 13-2

Voting 15-4, 21-7

W

Welcome
- example flipchart 23-11
- letter 12-2, 12-3, 23-21

WII-FM 17-9
Win-win 15-5, 16-2
Worksheet for meeting with leader 11-3

Y

Yosemite National Park i-7